WHAT IS A BISHOP?

IS VOLUME

83

OF THE

Twentieth Century Encyclopedia of Catholicism

UNDER SECTION

VIII

THE ORGANIZATION OF THE CHURCH

IT IS ALSO THE

91ST

VOLUME IN ORDER OF PUBLICATION

THE TWENTIETH CENTURY ENCYCLOPEDIA · OF CATHOLICISM

Edited by HENRI DANIEL-ROPS of the Académie Française

WHAT IS A BISHOP?

By JOSEPH URTASUN

Translated from the French by P. J. HEPBURNE-SCOTT

HAWTHORN BOOKS · PUBLISHERS · *New York*

First Edition, August, 1962

CONTENTS

INTRODUCTION

Questionnaires are now the fashion, and they can produce valuable results, when they are put methodically and conscientiously to competent and, above all, sincere persons. A book of this size cannot claim to be exhaustive in its scope, but let us question our contemporaries; what do they think of the bishop?

The heads of dioceses are certainly much less inaccessible than were their predecessors. Making use of modern means of transport, they are present at many gatherings and mix with the people. Except where persecution and offensiveness are the rule (as in nearly one-third of the world), they are even to be seen at official functions. And it is surely a good thing for the members of the ecclesiastical hierarchy to maintain courteous relations with the civil and military authorities, provided this does not give an impression of compromised loyalties, which would be harmful to both parties. Alongside, then, with the representatives of authority and the elected bodies, the man in the street may see a person dressed in black and purple, but the man in the street, whether baptized or not, is not always very profound in his judgements. Hatred perhaps prompts adverse opinions: Why is the bishop there? But people are often glad of his presence. One has only to look in their eyes to be sure of that. This is specially true when there has been some disaster, and a father comes to share the sorrow of his spiritual family. At such a time faith often revives, sympathy is more active. Sorrow, painful as it is, gives people a truer view of things, helps them better to penetrate the inmost hearts of others.

The non-Christian scarcely understands anything about the bishop. Looking at him from outside, he sees in him a person of greater or smaller influence, a sort of departmental head over the priests, entitled to give dispensations from the laws regulating marriages, burials, etc., able to pull strings to obtain some advantage or avoid some inconvenience. Among the different social classes, what hasty and opposed judgements are found! One set accuses the bishops of being hand in glove with the rich and the employers, another calls them demagogues when they defend the poor and the workers. The enemies of the Church, whether they appreciate or discredit his personal qualities, are afraid of the power of her chief representative. He will be as readily accused of interfering in politics as of excessive prudence and reserve. This is not surprising: the disciple is not above his Master.

What is more surprising is the ignorance of the faithful, of practising Catholics. To be sure, they have learnt in their catechism that the priest is the minister of Jesus Christ, that he depends on the bishop, who is subject to the pope. But too often, with an incomplete and erroneous notion of the Church, forgetting that they are part of her and have an active duty to evangelize, Catholics have only the vaguest ideas on the episcopate. Let the bishop, they think, write his long and not very thrilling letters to his people, or those rather frequent communications, all too often begging for money! But, except in country parishes, where it is the tradition to turn out in force for the children's confirmation, nobody bothers to go to the functions presided over by the bishop, incomprehensible as they seem, with all those ceremonial honours paid to his Lordship! It is enough for them to be present, with a certain pious curiosity, at his solemn enthronement or, better still, at his solemn funeral, or on other very special occasions.

This is true of the majority, including even those whose education and privileged position should give them a truer idea of the mission entrusted to the successor of St Peter and the apostles. Which of them reads and takes in either the pope's encyclicals or the declarations of the bishops? How few come into direct touch with their bishop, to give him information, to talk with him and receive his instructions?

The "militants" of Catholic Action have begun to realize how mistaken is this attitude. They feel the need to discuss things with their chief pastor, who commissions their own chaplains and gives them their own mandate to evangelize. How enriching this contact is to either party! The layman feels that he too is a part of the Church.

To the nuns the bishop is truly the one who represents Christ, and whom they love to receive, in spite of all the elaborate preparations for his visit. More and more, these consecrated souls seek to offer their intentions and prayers and acts of devotion in a generous spirit of collaboration. There has been great progress here, and there will be more.

The clergy, at least, should surely be united with him whose task they share. In every walk of life there is room for improvement in our ways of thought, speech and behaviour. Don't we all tend to judge without knowing all the facts, to pass from joking to criticism, without in any way meaning to fail in that admirable loyalty which is the boast of the priesthood as a whole? The clergy complain, and justifiably, of their isolation in the country parishes, but also of overwork in the town ministry. They should be better able to understand the rôle of the bishop, father, defender and friend of those "other selves" of his, the sharers in his priesthood, his indispensable fellow-workers among the flock committed to their common care. Nowadays it is easier than it used to be to meet together. This will greatly assist the full development of the priest's soul, as it enters more and more into the preoccupations of the chief pastor, the chief missionary of the whole diocese.

The bishops themselves, living in an age of constant exchanges, throughout their country and all over the world, are continually meeting one another. Abandoning the too limited outlook of their nineteenth-century predecessors, they now combine in order to give better service. The forthcoming Council will be a magnificent opportunity to demonstrate to the world the catholicity of the Church, under the authority of the vicar of Jesus Christ. May the unity that our Saviour prayed for after the Last Supper be realized! Let that be the object of all our prayers and endeavours!

It is our hope that these pages may be of some help to that end.

CHAPTER I

THE SUCCESSOR OF THE APOSTLES

It is all too easy to think of the Church as we think of an earthly State. Seen thus, the bishops, under the sovereignty of the pope, are merely so many lieutenants in purple, having under them various grades of officials who perform the priestly ministry and the services attached to it. The Church is indeed a visible society. But if we cannot distinguish it from every other kind of human authority, not only by its particular aim but by its supernatural constitution, we shall never understand it.

Mysterium Fidei, the mystery of faith: these words are added in the Mass to the words of consecration. The presence of Christ in the Blessed Sacrament remains inaccessible to those who judge only by appearances. It is the same with his eternal indwelling in the mystical Body of which he is the Head, and with the mission entrusted by him to the pope and the bishops.

THE CHURCH OF THE INCARNATE WORD AND HIS VICAR

When we consider the plan of divine Providence for mankind, we are filled with wonder at the sight of all the marvels before our eyes. But there is one work which sums up and, as it were, concentrates in itself everything great and beneficent wrought by God. This masterwork is the Church, the supernatural society instituted to hand down to men, through the ages, the truth once revealed and to apply to their souls the fruits of the redemption. To the Church our Lord has bequeathed not only his teaching, the dogmatic and moral truths which are to be the light of our minds and the rule of our conduct, but the divine channels through which the Blood shed on Calvary is poured out on us, and the worship which enables us, weak and miserable redeemed creatures, to render to God the homage due to him, till the consummation of the ages. More, Jesus Christ has entrusted his very self to the Body of which he is the Head, putting himself into its hands by the institution of the Blessed Sacrament, living in it by his grace and continual assistance. As Bossuet says, the Church is in very truth "Jesus Christ spread abroad and communicated" (Fourth letter to a lady of Metz). "Christ is the head of the Church", says St Paul; as a husband, "Christ shewed love to the Church when he gave himself up on its behalf. He would hallow it, purify it, ... it was to be holy, it was to be spotless" (Ephes. 4. 23–6).

But, faced with the forces of evil and the frailties of its members, how can the Church survive and develop till the end of time, guiding the successive generations on the road that leads to eternity? St Irenaeus gives the answer: "Where the Church is, there is the Spirit of God, and where the Spirit of God is, there is all grace" (*Adversus haereses,* III, 24). When God creates a work, he imprints his own mark on it. The three Persons of the Holy Trinity are but a single God. Between them, equal by their eternal substance, there is no distinction save in their interior relations, which are the source of fruitfulness and love in their unity. Nothing is more in accordance with the divine ideas than order. Order established between several is called hierarchy, for only by subordination can plurality be reduced to the unity which order demands.

The supreme Head of the Church is none other than Jesus Christ, the incarnate Word, who came down from heaven to bind together in one the scattered members of the great human family (John 11. 52). His presence is invisible, but does not a visible society need a Head who can be seen and heard? If the mass of the faithful had to obey only the hidden action of Christ, division would soon sow disturbance and doubt. That is why our Lord chose for himself a vicar: "Simon, son of Jona, ... thou art Peter, and it is upon this rock that I will build my church; and the gates of hell shall not prevail against it; and I will give to thee the keys of the kingdom of heaven; and whatever thou shalt bind on earth shall be bound in heaven" (Matt. 16. 17–19). And after the resurrection the Lord Jesus, letting him redeem the threefold denial by a triple affirmation of love, solemnly fulfilled his promise by giving Peter this order: "Feed my lambs, feed my sheep" (John 21. 15–17). The privilege of infallibility is granted to one who has not only the primacy of honour but a sovereignty over the universal Church: "I have prayed for thee, that thy faith may not fail; when, after a while, thou hast come back to me, it is for thee to be the support of thy brethren" (Luke 22. 32).

And let no one say, writes Bossuet, let no one think that St Peter's ministry ended with him! What is needed to uphold a universal Church can never have an end. Peter will live on in his successor. Peter will always speak from his Chair (*Sermon on the Unity of the Church*). (A splendid statement by this dazzling orator, who had not the same sureness of touch when he defended Gallicanism!) My own city of Avignon has had the honour, unchallenged by any other, even the most famous of capitals, of being the residence of seven lawful Roman pontiffs. One of the most celebrated was John XXII, the last John before our beloved common father today. This second Rome, indefectibly attached to the centre of Catholicism, is proud to proclaim that the Avignon popes did much for the Holy See and the honour of the Church.

We are all happy to repeat the words, almost literally quoted from St Cyprian, which gleam in letters of gold on the dome of the Vatican: *Hinc una fides mundo refulget, hinc sacerdotii unitas exoritur* (*Fourth Epistle to St Cornelius*). It is from the Chair of Peter, as from its hearth, that the one faith shines out on the world: it is from there, as from its root, that the episcopal college derives its authority.

And this is what the same great bishop of Carthage asserts:

> Christ builds his Church upon one man, and to him he commits his sheep to feed. To manifest the unity which must reign in Christian society, he established one chair, and laid down by his authority that this unity took its origin from one alone. . . . Certainly the other apostles were, like Peter, endowed with the same honours and powers; but all begins from unity, and the primacy is given to Peter, to show that the Church is one and that there is only one chair . . . (St Cyprian, *De Catholicae Ecclesiae Unitate*).

The first Vatican Council confirmed the universal and perpetual supremacy and the infallibility of the successor of Peter (Session 4). It was not untimely to remind men that the Church is built on this unshakable rock. The cornerstone is Christ, whose place is held by his vicar, but the whole building is founded on the apostles (Ephes. 2. 20).

THE MISSION OF THE APOSTLES

St Peter is the chief of the Twelve. The others, together with him, form the apostolic College. They too heard the words of power: "All authority in heaven and on earth has been given to me; you, therefore, must go out, making disciples of all nations, and baptizing them in the name of the Father, and of the Son, and of the Holy Ghost, teaching them to observe all the commandments which I have given you. And behold I am with you all through the days that are coming, until the consummation of the world" (Matt. 28. 18–20).

That is the source of their mission. The Son, in his Incarnation, is sent by the Father. The Church is mankind, embraced, assumed and transformed by him into the fellowship of the Father and of his Son Jesus Christ, as St John expresses it (1 John 1. 1–3). The Spirit in his turn, sent by the Father and the Son, comes to bring this work to perfection. In the words of St Peter Damian: "The Spirit penetrates and enlightens the Church, raising from it to God the tender appeals of filial love: Abba, Father" (Rom. 8. 15; Gal. 4).

Jesus Christ, the Word made man, sends out the apostles. He establishes the episcopal college and order, in which the universal Church subsists, as in its principal part. "As my Father has sent me, I am sending you out in my turn" (John 20. 21). "He who gives you welcome, gives me welcome too" (Matt. 10. 40). Christ will teach all truth (John 15. 15): he is the source of all grace and all authority: through his Spirit he gives light and communicates grace, and has appointed his apostles to govern the Church of God (Acts 20. 28). When they have received the outpouring of Pentecost they are filled with new strength, and will be witnesses to the ends of the inhabited world.

The apostles chosen by our Lord himself, with Matthias,

who at Peter's proposal filled the place of Judas, and Paul the "apostle of the Gentiles", certainly had the personal privileges of infallibly proclaiming revelation, of promulgating certain sacraments, of jurisdiction over the whole world. As a careful theologian has rightly said, the hierarchical powers are the means by which God *founded* the Church and *preserved* it. The power of Order, received in its fullness directly from Christ, was possessed equally by Peter and by the other apostles. Their "extraordinary jurisdiction" as founders was the same in each of them, but their "ordinary jurisdiction" had to be exercised under the authority of Peter, the sole shepherd of *all* the sheep, the rock on which the building rests. It is his supreme power which will ensure the *unity* of the Church, while the other apostles, and later their successors, will plant it in all parts of the world.

THE APOSTOLIC AGE

Marvel of marvels! The Holy Spirit, through the apostles, fills the whole known world. With the courage of which we read in the Acts, the Epistles and the Apocalypse, they proclaim everywhere the word of God. "It is impossible for us to refrain from speaking of what we have seen and heard" (Acts 4. 20). All of them, even John the beloved apostle, who took Mary into his keeping (John 19. 27), drank of the cup which Jesus promised them (Matt. 20. 22). They bore witness by martyrdom and died.

Over the Churches founded by them, the apostles placed "elders" and "overseers", though it is hard to say whether these presbyter-bishops had the fullness of the priesthood or not. It is worth noticing that in the Bible the presbyters are always mentioned in the plural, except in St John's Second and Third Epistles, where he calls himself by that name, but the bishop is named in the singular, except in

Acts 20. 28 and Phil. 1. 1. In his book in this series *What is a Priest?* Fr Lécuyer, an expert on the priesthood and the episcopate, gives all possible meanings of the word *episkopos*, "overseer". Passing over its application to magistrates, military commanders and overseers of works —and Numbers 4. 20, where the reference is to Eleazar's task of *watching over* the whole Tabernacle and everything in it—we may confine ourselves to the New Testament. The title is used for Christ himself (1 Peter, 2. 25). It is used in 1 Tim. 3. 1: "When a man aspires to a bishopric (*episkopé*), it is no mean employment that he covets." Timothy is reminded of his responsibilities and obligations, "remembering how prophecy singled thee out, long ago", following the intervention of the "prophets" on the occasion of his investiture by the Apostle. He is pastor of a community in which liturgical prayer holds a prominent place. In 2 Timothy St Paul exhorts him thus: "I would remind thee to fan the flame of that special grace which God kindled in thee *when my hands were laid upon thee*" (2 Tim. 1. 6). "A special grace has been entrusted to thee; prophecy awarded it, and the imposition of the presbyters' hands went with it; do not let it suffer from neglect. . . . Two things claim thy attention, thyself and the teaching of the faith; spend thy care on them; so wilt thou and those who listen to thee achieve salvation" (1 Tim. 4. 14–16). St Paul was a member of this college of presbyters, for in the former passage he spoke only of himself. The laying on of hands is not a mere blessing; it is the rite by which a grace is transmitted. It is used for the appointment of priests, and so is not to be used inconsiderately (1 Tim. 5. 22). It is the same for Titus in Crete (Titus 1. 5 and following), who will have to choose presbyters, and among them the bishop, God's steward, who must be undaunted, devoted to sound teaching, faithful to the doctrine.

In Galatians (1. 19), St Paul relates that he went up to Jerusalem to visit Cephas: "I did not see any of the other apostles, except James, the Lord's brother." James was the head of the local Church of Jerusalem, the successor in some sense of the Jewish high priest, and was succeeded by Simon.

At the beginning of the Apocalypse, St John addresses the "angel" of each of the seven Churches. The angels in heaven are of course their protectors and their "stars", but reproaches could not be levelled against them, so the word must surely mean those who ruled these communities.

At the close of the first century St Clement of Rome sent a letter to the Corinthians. "The apostles received for us the Gospel from the Lord Jesus Christ. Jesus the Christ was sent by God. So the Christ came from God and the apostles from the Christ" (42. 1). The apostles set about preaching the Gospel. They appointed bishops and deacons among those who were to believe.

The apostles knew that there would be disputes about authority in the Church. "For this cause, therefore, having received complete foreknowledge, they appointed the aforesaid persons and afterwards they established a rule, that if these should fall asleep, other approved men should succeed to their ministration" (44. 2).

St Irenaeus was a disciple of St Polycarp, a bishop of Smyrna who had known St John. He asserts that the doctrine of the apostles has come down to us "through the succession of the bishops" (*Adversus haereses*, 3, 3, 1; Harvey's edn., II, pp. 8–9).

THE PRIESTHOOD IN ITS FULLNESS

The bishops are the heirs of the apostles as regards the priesthood. Christ is the one eternal Priest according to the order of Melchisedech (Ps. 109), offering the bread and the wine, mediator of the New Covenant sealed by his blood. "The purpose for which any high priest is chosen from among his fellow-men and made a representative of men in their dealings with God, is to offer gifts and sacrifices in expiation of their sins" (Hebr. 5. 1).

For a long time the word *sacerdos* meant the bishop: for a presbyter the words *secundi ordinis*, "of the second rank", were added. Tertullian calls the bishop *summus sacerdos*, the high priest. In Christian antiquity it is he who celebrates the eucharistic sacrifice surrounded by his *presbyterium*, or college of presbyters. He teaches with the authority which comes to him from the apostles: he imparts to his fellow-workers the power to baptize, to absolve, to administer the other sacraments.

The dignity of the episcopate, started precisely by St Ignatius of Antioch and St Cyprian, was made illustrious by generations of great bishops, pioneers and teachers of the faith against heresies, defenders of the city against the barbarian invasion. Then, under worldly influences, the glory of the episcopal college suffered eclipse, and in the Middle Ages, at least in western regions, its activity was less pure, less radiant.

THE EPISCOPATE AS A SACRAMENT

Although in the East the question was never raised, it was debated in the West whether the episcopate was really a sacrament, distinct from the presbyterate, or whether the distinction between them was based only on a difference of jurisdiction. (Its apostolic authority was never disputed.) Under Pope Damasus the deacons of Rome had acquired such importance that they thought themselves above ordinary priests. To refute their claims, St Jerome and a Roman author known to us as Ambrosiaster tried to assimilate the episcopate to the priesthood, in respect of the sacrament of Order.

St Thomas Aquinas, when he began his teaching in Paris, had to expound the book of *Sentences* of Peter Lombard, according to whom the episcopate is neither an order nor a sacrament. His master St Albert the Great, like pseudo-Dionysius, maintained on the contrary that the episcopate was an order superior to the presbyterate, not in the consecration of the Eucharist, but in relation to the mystical Body. A special grace makes the bishop able to rule the people of God in the name of Christ. He is the "ordinary minister" (that is, by right of his office) of Confirmation and Order, for these sacraments bestow a special rôle to perform in the Body of Christ, which is the Church. Also, in so far as the Eucharist has for its fruit the unity of the mystical Body, the simple priest is dependent on the episcopal college.

The Council of Trent merely defined the existence in the Church of the divinely instituted hierarchy, composed of bishops, priests and ministers, and the superiority over simple priests of the bishops, who have the "ordinary power" of conferring Confirmation and Order (Session 23). Then, after a long silence, the theology of the episcopate was studied by Bouix in an excellent canonical treatise, and by Dom Gréa, founder and abbot general of the Canons Regular of the Immaculate Conception, in his book *De l'Eglise et sa divine constitution*. This important point of doctrine has now been explored in numerous essays and books, notably by Mgr Charles Journet in volume I of *The Church of the Incarnate Word*.

Admittedly, by special delegation and in special circumstances, ordinary priests have received, and do receive, the faculty to administer the sacrament of Confirmation; prefects apostolic, and parish priests in their parishes for those in danger of death.

The recent discovery of papal Bulls of the fifteenth

century, giving Cistercian abbots the exceptional faculty
to ordain even priests has caused surprise, but no example
is known of a priest consecrating a bishop. A large number
of authorities on this subject agree that the episcopate is
truly a sacrament. Is it not an outward sign, instituted
by Christ, producing grace and the fullness of the priesthood? Simple deacons have been consecrated bishops
without first receiving priestly ordination, as was the case
with several popes. But why should episcopal consecration give grace and bestow character only when the re-
cipient is not yet a priest?

On June 5th, 1960, the present Pope, after enthroning
fourteen new bishops, consecrated by himself, for missionary lands, declared as follows in his allocution:

> Here we see renewed one of the most moving scenes in
> the life of Christ, the apostolic mandate—committed to
> Peter and the first apostles, to go into all the world and
> preach the Gospel to all nations. The humble successor of
> Peter, surrounded by the elders of the Church, repeats,
> though in a different form, the original invocation: *he
> renews the act which conveys the episcopal character and
> grace.* Beloved brothers and sons who have just been con-
> secrated, the title which will henceforth be added to your
> surname, *humilis episcopus Ecclesiae Dei,* humble bishop
> of the Church of God, now suffices to confer on you the
> highest honour for time and for eternity (*Osservatore
> Romano,* June 9th, 1960; *Documentation Catholique,* 1329,
> July 5th, 1960).

What an honour, what a responsibility, to become a successor of the Twelve, to be in our time, as in times past,
a perpetuator of their mission! "Keep watch, then, over
yourselves, and over God's Church, in which the Holy
Spirit has made you bishops; you are to be the shepherds
of that flock which he won for himself at the price of his
own blood" (Acts 20. 28).

CHAPTER II

THE BISHOP IN UNION WITH THE POPE AND THE OTHER BISHOPS

Before considering the bishop as the head of his diocese, it will be well to define his relations, first with the pope, then with his brethren in the episcopate.

THE EPISCOPAL COLLEGE

When the apostles reached the end of their mortal lives, cut short by the hatred of Christ's enemies, they had men to replace them in the exercise of their ordinary power. The apostolic college, presided over by Peter, was in time replaced by the episcopal college which, under the authority of the pope, forms part of the very constitution of the Church. Institutions of a merely ecclesiastical order may disappear, despite the immense harm which may result thereby to the expansion of Christianity, but so long as mankind survives, there will be bishops. They are not mere delegates of the pope, though they are directly chosen by him.

SUBJECT TO THE SUCCESSOR OF PETER

The bishop of Rome has immediate, episcopal and supreme jurisdiction over the whole world. Peter received his authority from Christ, directly and independently of the Twelve. Vicar of Jesus Christ on earth, he is the foundation and the visible Head of the Church, which must endure till the end of time. The prince of the apostles holds the power, symbolized by the keys, of binding and loosing. Whoever lawfully succeeds him in his see inherits his primacy. That is a dogma founded on Scripture and constant tradition.

The supremacy of the pope extends to each and all of the faithful, each and all of the pastors. Leo XIII thus expressed it in his encyclical *Satis Cognitum,* of June 29th, 1896.

But the order of bishops could not be regarded as truly united to Peter, in the manner willed by Christ, if it were not subject to Peter and united to him; otherwise it would inevitably be broken up into a multitude, full of confusion and disorder. To preserve the unity of faith and communion as it should be, neither a primacy of honour nor a power of direction is sufficient; there must necessarily be an authority which is real and also sovereign, obeyed by the whole community. When the Son of God committed the keys of the kingdom of God to Peter alone, what was his purpose? Biblical usage and the unanimous consent of the Fathers put it beyond doubt that the keys here signify the supreme power. No other interpretation can be given of the powers conferred on Peter separately or on the apostles conjointly with him. If the power of binding and loosing, and of feeding the flock, gives to the bishops, as successors of the apostles, the right to govern each his own diocese with a real authority, certainly this same power must produce the same effect in him to whom God himself has assigned the rôle of feeding the lambs and the sheep.

Peter was appointed by Christ to be, not only the shepherd, but the shepherd of the shepherds. Peter therefore feeds both the lambs and the sheep; he feeds the little ones and the mothers; he rules the subjects and also rules the prelates, for in the Church, apart from the lambs and the sheep, there is nothing (St Bruno, bishop of Segni, *Comm. in Joann.* 3, 21, 55).

Hence we find in the Fathers those quite special expressions which denote the blessed Peter and show him clearly to be placed at the supreme point of dignity and power. They call him, in one place or another, the head of the assembly of the apostles; the prince of the holy apostles: the leader of the apostolic choir: the mouthpiece of all the apostles: the head of this family: he who commands the whole world: the first among the apostles: the pillar of the Church.

It is the pope who nominates the bishops—we shall see later how he does so. As vicegerent of Christ he "confirms his brethren", he is the principle of unity for all the members of the body of the Church, the upholder and defender of the rights of the bishops.

UNION BETWEEN THE SUCCESSORS
OF THE APOSTLES

The number of bishops ever increases with the spread of Catholicism and the establishment of the hierarchy in new lands. But they form, like their first predecessors, a single college, welded together by the intimate bond of the same faith and the same charity which the Holy Spirit has shed abroad in their hearts (John 17. 11, 21, 22).

We should not forget the enlightening instructions of Pius XII on their function as the "first of the Lord's members" (*Mystici Corporis,* June 29th, 1943). He spoke forcibly about the Magisterium (teaching office) which belongs to the bishops, while encouraging the studies of the theologians who are subject to them. He recalled the principles of episcopal government, which extends to everything directly or indirectly concerned with dogma and morals (Discourses of May 31st and November 2nd, 1954).

Important teaching was given in the encyclical *Fidei Donum*:

> Certainly it was to the apostle Peter alone, and to his successors the Roman pontiffs, that Jesus entrusted the whole of his flock. But while each bishop is the peculiar pastor only of that portion of the flock entrusted to his charge, his character as lawful successor of the apostles by divine institution makes him jointly responsible for the apostolic mission of the Church, according to the saying of Christ to his apostles: As the Father has sent me, even so I send you. This mission, which must embrace all nations and all ages, has not ceased with the death of the apostles: it continues in the person of all the bishops in communion with the vicar of Jesus Christ. In them, who are supremely the envoys, the missionaries of the Lord, resides in its fullness the dignity of the episcopate, which is the highest in the Church, as St Thomas Aquinas declares (Commentary on Romans, 1. 1), and it is from their hearts that the apostolic fire, brought to earth by Christ, must be communicated to the hearts of all our sons and inspire in them a new ardour for the missionary action of the Church in the world.

Evangelization is an essentially corporate work. In the beginning it was done by "Peter and his companions" (Mark 1. 36; Luke 9. 32; 8. 45). The name of apostle was extended, in the famous phrase of Eusebius, to "those evangelizers who held the first rank in their succession".

EPISCOPAL CONSECRATION

The bishops in communion with Peter's successor are corporately charged to carry the Gospel into all the world.

This is emphasized by the ceremonial of episcopal consecration. After the reading of the apostolic mandate and
the oath of fidelity, there follows the examination on the
purpose of obedience and on faith in the articles of the
Catholic creed. Then, in the course of the Mass, the consecrator and his two co-consecrators place the open book
of the Gospels on the head and shoulders of the candidate
(in which position it is held by one of the acolytes) before
laying on their hands and pronouncing aloud: *Accipe
Spiritum Sanctum:* "Receive the Holy Ghost". The Consecration Preface prays for grace to be given to the one
chosen by God to exercise the supreme priesthood: "Perfect in thy priest the fullness of thy ministry and, clothing
him in all the ornaments of spiritual glorification, sanctify
him with the heavenly anointing". After these words,
which are the "sacramental form" (Constitution of November 30th, 1947), the solemn prayer continues:

> In his preaching, may he never employ the language of
> human wisdom to persuade, but rely on the manifestation
> of the Spirit and the power of God. May he who curses
> him be accursed, and he who obeys him be abundantly
> blessed. May he be that good and faithful servant appointed
> by thee, O Lord, over thy household, to give them their
> portion of meat in due season and make all men perfect.
> Outwardly unwearied in all his duties, may he inwardly
> guard strength of soul. May he hate pride and love humility
> and truth, never forsaking them for love of praise or for
> any motive of fear. May he never set darkness in place of
> light, nor light in place of darkness. May he never give evil
> the name of good, nor good the name of evil. May he
> know that he is answerable to the wise and to the foolish,
> to the learned and to the ignorant, that he may draw profit
> from the advancement of all (*Roman Pontifical*, Consecra-
> tion of Bishops).

By the collective action of his colleagues the new bishop
is incorporated into the order of bishops. Henceforth he

will ensure the stability and growth of the mystical Body which is the Church of Jesus Christ, the sole Supreme Priest. The fullness of the priesthood consists in carrying out, in Christ's name, the mission of ruling, sanctifying and teaching the flock. Infallibility, of course, does not belong to each individual bishop, but to the whole episcopate united with the pope. He must build up the Church, relying on our Lord's promises of perpetuity, and on his prayer for those who should believe in him through the apostles' word (John 17. 9).

The power of Order belonging to the apostles and the bishops is equal to that of Peter and the pope. Under the pope's leadership, the episcopate is the same for all bishops, whether they occupy great sees or small, or even have no diocese to rule. The last, formerly called bishops *in partibus infidelium* (heathen lands), are now called titular bishops. Their title of archbishop or bishop is that of some historic local Church. This is the position of apostolic nuncios and delegates, of coadjutors with right of succession, of auxiliary bishops without that right, of vicars apostolic, and of other dignitaries who are in episcopal orders.

Only the pope can create a hierarchy among the bishops. Apart from the dignity of the cardinalate, which did not hitherto necessarily involve episcopal Orders (the cardinal deacons used not to be bishops) there are still some distinctions of rank to be noted. Highest of all are the patriarchs, who have immense influence and undisputed authority in the East, not only over the patriarchal diocese, but over the bishops, priests and faithful of their rite. The position of primate, even when recognized by the Holy See, carries dignity but rarely any special authority. The metropolitans, in circumstances laid down by canon law, enjoy a degree of precedence in their ecclesiastical provinces. Within this area they have the privilege of having the archiepiscopal cross carried before them, and of wearing (during pontifical Masses on certain feasts) the *pallium*, a plain band of white wool adorned with black crosses, which the pope has blessed and sent to them. The local Ordinary (*Ordinarius loci*), that is, the bishop of the diocese, takes precedence of all other bishops, with the exception of cardinals, the apostolic nuncio or delegate and his own archbishop. Certain archbishops and bishops are appointed assistants at the papal throne; in the papal chapels they take precedence over all other bishops. But the external side of ecclesiastical dignities matters little. The pomp is for the sake of the people who take part in the ceremonies, not for the bishop, a poor sinner who is bowed down under it all. "The Word of God", says St Gregory the Great in his seventeenth Homily, "is handed on, and can only be handed on to men when it springs from charity and passes through charity. The apostolate must therefore spring from an entire and wholly mutual charity."

EPISCOPAL MEETINGS

The unity of the episcopate is a necessity for the evangelization of distant peoples: that is proved by the links between ancient and modern Churches. It is shown by a common concern for national or regional apostolate. Never have there been so many gatherings of bishops governed by mutual understanding and a concern for a coordinated line of conduct—though it need not be uniform, for circumstances differ.

Apart from various informal meetings of the bishops in a particular region or country, and from the diocesan synod, which is summoned by a diocesan bishop every ten years and in which he is the sole legislator, there are two sorts of solemn and formal meetings of members of the hierarchy[1] and these are what are known as plenary councils and provincial councils. A few words may be said about each of these.

PLENARY COUNCILS

The first and more important is the plenary council, which is defined and discussed in the code of canon law in two of its canons (281 and 282). In the first canon it is enacted that the Ordinaries of several ecclesiastical provinces may unite in a plenary council, provided that the leave of the Holy See has been obtained, when the pope will appoint a legate to summon and preside over the council. It is agreed by canonists that there is no obligation to meet in plenary councils, and that, according to the Church's law, there is no *permanent* ecclesiastical jurisdiction to be found intermediately between the pope and the metropolitans of the various provinces. Councils of this plenary nature have been held frequently in the Church's history. The first in the West was the Council of Arles (314), and in the East the Council of Sardica (343). Canon 282 enumerates the prelates to be summoned to such a gathering. These include, in addition to the papal legate, the metropolitans, the diocesan bishops, administrators apostolic of dioceses, vicars and prefects apostolic, and the vicars capitular having rule over dioceses during a vacancy. Titular bishops, who are resident in the territory, may be summoned by the papal legate to attend the plenary council. If they attend they are, in default of

[1] More correctly one might say "the principal members of the hierarchy," since, according to the Council of Trent's 23rd Session (on the sacrament of holy Orders) the hierarchy consists not of bishops alone, but of bishops, priests and deacons (Cf. Denzinger's *Enchiridion Symbolorum*, sections 960 and 966).

any contrary decision by the council, entitled to a deliberative, or fully effective, vote. All other persons summoned
(e.g. theologians, canonists and religious superiors) may
be consulted, but have no effective vote.

PROVINCIAL COUNCILS

A provincial council is one that is summoned, normally
by the metropolitan of a province, and is attended by all
the bishops of the province. It should take place at intervals of not more than twenty-five years (can. 582).
Normally it is presided over by the archbishop of the province, and, though this latter point is not strictly determined, it is usually to be held in the metropolitan cathedral
(can. 284, sect. 1). A rather lengthy canon (285) decides
that bishops who have no metropolitan, archbishops without suffragans, and some lesser prelates may, with leave
from the Holy See, choose, once for all, the province to
which they wish to be attached for the purpose of a provincial council. The regulations about titular bishops residing in the province are on the same lines as those for the
plenary councils (can. 286, sect. 2).

Cathedral chapters, or (in dioceses without canons) diocesan consultors, are to be invited to the council and, after
receiving the invitation, are to choose two of their number
to take part in the proceedings. These delegates may be
consulted, but have no deliberative vote (can. 286, sect. 3).

Canon 287 is concerned with the sending of proxies by
those who have a full vote, but are lawfully hindered from
coming in person. According to canon 288 it is for the
presiding bishop in plenary and provincial councils to
decide the order of the questions to be discussed. Once
the council has begun, nobody may leave except for a
good reason to be approved by the legate or the fathers

of the council (can. 289). The acts of the council are to be sent to Rome, and may not be published until they have been approved by the Sacred Congregation of the Consistorial. Once promulgated they bind all those in a province or group of provinces. An individual bishop may dispense from a decree only in a particular case and for a sufficient reason.

THE ECUMENICAL COUNCIL

On January 25th, 1959, our present Holy Father decreed the convocation of an Ecumenical Council, the twenty-first in order, to be held at St Peter's in Rome and named the Second Council of the Vatican. It will be under the patronage of the Blessed Virgin Mary and the protection of St Joseph, and will open in the course of 1962.

A preliminary commission has consulted the bishops, the general superiors of the religious orders, and the Catholic universities. Its president was the late Cardinal Tardini. All the answers have been classified and printed. Eight quarto volumes of from 800 to 1,000 pages are devoted to the suggestions of the episcopate alone.

The preparatory phase was opened by the pope on November 24th, 1960. The Central Commission is presided over by the Holy Father himself, and its Secretary-General is H.E. Mgr Felici, titular archbishop of Samosata. It is composed of cardinals, archbishops and bishops from the whole world, and notably of the presidents of the episcopal colleges of the various countries.

The eleven preparatory commissions, each presided over by a cardinal, are as follows:

1. The theological commission, to examine questions on Holy Scripture, tradition, faith and morals (*President*: Cardinal Ottaviani, Secretary of the Holy Office; *Secretary*: Fr Tromp, S.J., a German).

2. Commission on bishops and the government of dioceses (*Pres.,* Cardinal Marella; *Sec.,* Mgr Gawlina, titular archbishop of Madito, a Pole.)

3. Commission on the discipline of the clergy and laity (*Pres.,* Cardinal Ciriaci, Prefect of the Congregation of the Council; *Sec.,* Fr Berutti, O.P., an Italian.)

4. The commission on Religious (*Pres.,* Cardinal Valerio Valeri, Prefect of the Congregation of Religious; *Sec.,* Fr Rousseau, O.M.I., a Canadian).

5. Commission on the discipline of the Sacraments (*Pres.,* Cardinal Masella, Prefect of the Congregation of the Sacraments; *Sec.,* Fr Bidagor, S.J., a Spaniard).

6. Commission on the Liturgy (*Pres.,* Cardinal Larraona, Prefect of the Congregation of Rites; *Sec.,* Don Bugnini, C.M., an Italian).

7. Commission on Studies and Seminaries (*Pres.,* Cardinal Pizzardo, Prefect of the Congregation of Universities and Seminaries; *Sec.,* Dom Mayer, O.S.B., a German).

8. Commission on the Eastern Church (*Pres.,* Cardinal Amleto Cicognani, Secretary of the Congregation of the Eastern Church; *Sec.,* Fr Weylykyi, Basilian of St Josaphat, a Ukrainian).

9. Commission on the Missions (*Pres.,* Cardinal Agagianian, Prefect of the Congregation of Propaganda; *Sec.,* Mgr Mathew, titular archbishop of Apamea in Bithynia, an Englishman).

10. Commission on the apostolate of the laity, and all questions of Catholic Action, religious and social action (*Pres.,* Cardinal Cento; *Sec.,* Mgr Achille Glorieux, a Frenchman).

11. Commission on ceremonial (*Pres.,* Cardinal Tisserant; *Sec.,* Mgr Nardone, an Italian).

Each commission contains a score of members and the

same number of consultors, who are all experienced bishops, priests or religious.

There are three Secretariats. That for the Unity of Christians is presided over by Cardinal Bea, S.J., a German, and its Secretary is Mgr Willebrands, of the Netherlands. The president of the Secretariat for the press, radio, cinema and television is Mgr O'Connor, an American, and the Secretary is Mgr Deskar, from Poland. The Secretariat in charge of the economic and technical preparations for the Council is presided over by Cardinal di Jorio, and its Secretary is Mgr Guerri (Italian). This body includes laymen.

The following are summoned to the Council with the right to speak and vote: cardinals (even if not bishops), patriarchs, primates, resident archbishops and bishops, certain abbots and general superiors. Titular bishops (in episcopal orders but not in charge of a diocese), if they are summoned, have a deliberate vote. Being members of the episcopal college, they act as judges of faith and discipline, as Fathers of the Council.

On December 31st, 1961, the Sacred College was composed of 80 cardinals, six of whom were suburbicarian bishops, that is, bishops of certain sees near Rome. There were eleven patriarchs, besides five titular patriarchs. There were 345 metropolitan sees, 46 archbishoprics without ecclesiastical provinces, 1,370 residential episcopal sees. There were 972 titular archbishops and bishops, 98 prelates or abbots *nullius* (directly dependent on the Holy See), ten apostolic administrators. In addition there were 139 vicariates apostolic, 107 prefectures and six missions.

Theologians and canonists will render invaluable service, but only in a consultative capacity. In the "ordinary" *magisterium* the bishops in communion with the Holy See form the teaching Church. The "extraordinary" Magisterium may include other members taking part in their deliberations. The Supreme Pontiff grants a universal authority to its representatives, even when they are not in possession of episcopal dignity, just as the Church recognizes doctors who are not bishops.

The number attending the Council may perhaps reach 2,800, far higher than at any previous conciliar gatherings. But there are sure to be many unwilling absentees, owing to the risks of illness, but even more to the persecutions which hold captive the bishops of the "Church of Silence".

We give here the numbers of those who took part in former Ecumenical Councils.

Place	Date	Number of bishops
Nicaea I	325	319
Constantinople I	381	186
Ephesus	431	250
Chalcedon	451	600
Constantinople II	553	150
Constantinople III	680	174
Nicaea II	787	390
Constantinople IV	870	102
Lateran I	1123	300
Lateran II	1139	1000
Lateran III	1179	700
Lateran IV	1215	800
Lyons I	1245	140
Lyons II	1274	1000
Vienne	1312	300
Constance	1414–18	600
Florence	1438–45	200
Lateran V	1512–17	120
Trent	1545–63	255
Vatican I	1870	747

Some important studies have recently appeared on the General Council,[2] from the theological and historical points of view, and our readers would do well to consult them. It is certain that supreme and plenary power resides in the Roman pontiff alone, independently of any concerted action with the other bishops, its only limits being those of natural and divine law. Councils, therefore, are not strictly necessary. But their usefulness is great indeed, for the bishops, gathered with their head in Ecumenical Council, represent the whole Church and truly possess indisputable authority over it.

St Irenaeus ascribes to the bishop "a sure charisma of truth", like that which the apostles received on the day of Pentecost. This is referred to in the oath against modernism, when it affirms "that it is and always will be in the succession of the episcopate from the apostles". The bishops, especially in the Ecumenical Council, summoned, presided over and confirmed by the pope, are the authentic witnesses to the faith of their Churches, truly judges and teachers of the faith. They have authority to unmask error in enemies both without and within, to teach the truth from the most favourable points of view: doctrinal, pastoral and missionary.

What a magnificent vision of Epiphany, in the atmosphere of a new Pentecost, will be seen at the Second Council of the Vatican, with the Fathers of all races, all colours, all languages, heads of ancient Churches and of missions! It will illustrate the words of St Paul, Apostle of the Gentiles, to the Romans (10. 11–13): "Anyone who believes in him will not be disappointed. There is no distinction made between Jew and Gentile; all alike have one Lord, and he has enough and to spare for all those

[2] See, in this series, F. Dvornik, *The General Councils of the Church.*

who call upon him. Everyone who calls upon the name of the Lord will be saved."

The unity of the Church is an article of the Catholic faith, enshrined in the Nicene Creed which we recite at Mass every Sunday. It is one of the notes of the true Church of Christ. The unity of all Christians is, unhappily, far from being realized. May God make use of the approaching Council, to prepare for the reunion of those who have been separated for so many centuries! The Holy Father thus expressed his desire on February 21st, 1959: "May the One Holy Catholic Church be thereby enabled to set up a standard and also to speak out with a clear voice, inviting all those who boast the name of Christian, but have unhappily been separated in times past, to rejoin the flock of Christ" (Letter to the bishop of Trier).

The encyclical of June 29th in the same year laid down the intended aim of the Council: "the development of the Catholic faith, the moral renewal of the Christian life of the faithful, and adaptation to the needs and methods of our time". Let us open our minds to welcome the great decisions to be made, invoking the help of the Holy Spirit for the vicar of Christ and his venerable brethren in the episcopal order, from East and West alike.

Episcopalianism (the false theory that the college of bishops is above the pope) is an error rejected at the first Vatican Council, which was interrupted in 1870. We must equally reject every tendency to oppose the bishops to the pope, who honours them and defends them when they are attacked. Their security and their strength lie in their faithful attachment to Rome, which safeguards the unity of the universal Church.

CHAPTER III

THE BISHOP ACCORDING TO THE CODE OF CANON LAW

There are in the Church's code of canon law very numerous references to bishops, and to these the alphabetical index s.v. *Episcopi,* listing fifty or sixty items, is an inadequate guide. Cross-references indicate such subjects as the bestowal of benefices, church dignities, cathedral chapters, the sacred ministry and others. Yet the canons directly concerned with the episcopal office are few in number; there are exactly twenty-one of them (i.e. can. 329–49), which find a place between those dealing with vicars and prefects apostolic, and those concerned with auxiliary and coadjutor bishops. These twenty-one canons may be grouped under five headings: What is a bishop? How is a bishop appointed? What are his powers? What are his duties? What privileges has he? A sixth division might be: How can he resign the episcopal office? (No canon deals *ex professo,* it is true, with this last subject, but most authors agree that it can and should be discussed.)

WHAT IS A BISHOP?

The answer to this question is given in the first section of canon 329: "Bishops are successors to the apostles and are divinely instituted; they are set over particular churches, which they govern in virtue of ordinary power, under the authority of the Roman Pontiff." It is to be noted that they are styled successors of the apostles, but not successors of Christ. They have not all the spiritual privileges enjoyed by the apostles (e.g. they are not personally infallible), with the exception noted below, they have not universal jurisdiction in the Church, but in all essentials they have the same powers of sacred order and of jurisdiction as the original apostles. The divine institution of the episcopate is clearly laid down in that canon of the Council of Trent to which reference was made above (can. 6: Denzinger's *Enchiridion Symbolorum,* sect. 966): "If anyone shall affirm that there is not in the Catholic Church a hierarchy founded by divine institution, which is made up of bishops, priests and deacons, let him be anathema." The rule of all bishops, apart from the vicar of Christ himself, is limited to a particular territory. Moreover, the pope can limit the powers of bishops, for example, by reserving the absolution of certain sins to himself, but he cannot suppress episcopal power or radically change its character.

THE APPOINTMENT OF BISHOPS

The second section of canon 329 lays down the basic principle in this matter: "The Roman Pontiff freely names the bishops." In the earliest ages of the Church the apostles themselves chose their successors, and, by the time of the first Ecumenical Council of Nicaea (325) it was decided that the choice of candidates should be made by the bishops of a province and ratified by the metropolitan. In practice, at the present time, there are several methods by which the names of suitable candidates may be brought to the notice of the authorities in Rome. In England, where every diocese is provided with a cathedral chapter, the canons are permitted to send in names to be submitted to Rome, after the bishops of the province have had their say in the matter. In the United States the apostolic delegate submits names to the Holy See, after these have been discussed and voted upon by the bishops of each province, at meetings held at least every two years.[1]

The canon that follows (330) insists that, before a man can be raised to the episcopate, proof must be given, according to the method established by the apostolic see, that he is fit for the office. Information is accumulated about candidates through various channels, the whole process being carried out in complete secrecy.

The qualities required in a bishop are set out in canon 331. A candidate must be born in lawful wedlock; it is not sufficient that he should have been legitimated by the subsequent marriage of his parents. He must be not less than thirty years of age, and have been ordained priest for not less than five years. He must exhibit the qualities of integrity, piety, zeal for souls and prudence. He should hold the degree of doctor, or at the very least of licentiate, in theology or canon law. Failing this, he should be well informed as a theologian or canonist. A later section reserves all judgement about a candidate's fitness uniquely to the Holy See (can. 331, sect. 3).

[1] Cf. the decree *Ratio* of July 25th, 1916 (*Acta Apost. Sedis,* viii, 400 ff., printed in T. L. Bouscaren, *The Canon Law Digest,* i (Milwaukee, 1934), pp. 194–98). Very similar decrees govern the selection of candidates in other countries, e.g. Canada and Newfoundland, Scotland, Brazil, Mexico and Poland.

Even though, according to the custom in some countries, the candidate may have been presented to the Holy See for acceptance by some civil government, the actual institution or investiture belongs entirely to the vicar of Christ (can. 332, sect. 1). Before his investiture the candidate must make the profession of faith, together with an oath of loyalty to the apostolic see (can. 332, sect. 2).

The newly appointed bishop is obliged to receive episcopal consecration within three months after obtaining his letters of appointment; within four months of receiving the letters, he must proceed to his diocese (can. 333). His consecration must take place at the hands of some bishop in full communion with the Holy See; normally two other bishops must assist the consecrator, though on many occasions leave has been given, in case of real necessity, for two priests to take the place of the two co-consecrators. The penalties attached to any unauthorized episcopal consecrations have always been severe, and now are even more so. By a decree of the Holy Office, dated April 9th, 1951, both the consecrator and the new bishop incur excommunication most specially reserved to the Holy See. The code's legislation (can. 2370) originally prescribed the milder penalty of suspension from all episcopal functions for all concerned, including the co-consecrating assistants.

The chief effects of episcopal consecration are, first, the bestowal of the episcopal character, and, secondly, a close spiritual union between the new bishop and the diocese to which he has been assigned.

THE BISHOP'S POWERS

Can. 334, sect. 1, defines that "residential bishops are the ordinary and immediate pastors of the diocese committed to their charge". Their powers are styled *ordinary* because they are attached to the episcopate as of right, and not as a result of some form of delegation. They are *immediate,* because they are exercised without the need of any intermediary. They are not, however, *absolute* powers, and the bishop is bound by the canon law and by the obligations of his state, and must allow his priestly subjects reasonable freedom in the exercise of the jurisdiction accorded to them.

Before he can exercise his powers (can. 334, sect. 2), the bishop is obliged to take possession of his diocese by showing his letters of appointment to the chapter of the diocese (or, in the case of the United States, to the board of diocesan consultors). The secretary of the chapter or the chancellor of the diocese should be in attendance to make a record of the proceedings in the chapter's register. No special ceremony is prescribed; it is not even necessary that the new bishop should exhibit his letters in the chapter-house (can. 334, sect. 3).

The general powers exercised by bishops are stated clearly in can. 335, sect. 1. They have "the right and the duty to govern their dioceses in spiritual and temporal matters, with power that is legislative, judicial and coercive; such power is to be exercised in terms of the rules laid down by the sacred canons". In addition to the three types of power mentioned in the canon, the bishop has also the position of chief teacher of doctrine in the diocese, and the legal right to direct all administrative acts.

As regards the *judicial* and *coercive* powers the bishop is the ordinary judge, at first instance, in his own diocese (can. 1572) and has authority in regard to all cases that are not reserved to a still higher judge. He can exercise his judicial powers by means of the diocesan tribunal, presided over by the official, who acts in his name and with his authority. In the internal forum (of conscience) he has power to absolve from certain classes of reserved sins, as also from various censures.

His *doctrinal* authority is manifested in his own preaching (can. 1327), by his delegation of the mission to preach (can. 1337 and 1366) and by his vigilant care of every method of teaching sacred doctrine (can. 336 and 1366).

His powers as a *legislator* are set out in can. 335, sect 2. He may make laws for his own diocese either at the diocesan synod or in the course of pastoral visitation, or at other times. Such laws begin to take effect immediately after their promulgation; the mode of promulgating them is decided by the bishop himself. One important limitation to his power is that he may not forbid what is expressly permitted by the common law of the Church, nor may he allow what that common law forbids. He may, however, give particular application to a general law, e.g. by determining the time, place and other details of its incidence.

THE BISHOP'S DUTIES

Mention has already been made of the new bishop's duty of making the profession of faith and of taking an oath of loyalty to the Holy See.

A well-known manual states succinctly the chief duties of resident bishops. "The bishop's primary duties are to *govern the diocese,* see to the observance of the laws of the Church, prevent abuses, safeguard the purity of faith and morals, and promote Catholic education and Catholic Action (canons 335, 336)."[2]

These are all parts of the duty of vigilance. This duty is carried out not merely in the bishop's own preaching and his sharing of the teaching office with others. He has the obligation of watching over the literature concerned

[2] T. L. Bouscaren, S.J., and A. C. Ellis, S.J., *Canon Law: A Text and Commentary,* Milwaukee, 1955, p. 175.

with matters of faith and morals, and of forbidding the issue of any books that may convey false teaching.

In his exercise of the power of order, the bishop is entitled to carry out pontifical functions throughout the churches of the diocese or province, and this includes churches of exempt religious. He is not, however, entitled to exercise such functions outside his own diocese, except with leave from the local bishop, or, as regards exempt religious, from the religious superior (can. 337, sect. 1).

He is also both obliged and entitled to administer the sacraments throughout his diocese. As a diocesan bishop he has the ordinary power of conferring the sacraments of confirmation and of holy Order.

Certain sacramentals are reserved to him. He alone may normally consecrate the three oils (chrism, baptismal, and of the sick) used in the Church's rites, and may carry out blessings that require the use of holy oil, such as the consecration of patens and chalices, of bells, and of altars.

His duties also comprise vigilance regarding liturgical worship, the celebration of pontifical Mass on the greater feasts (can. 338) and the care and public exposition of the Blessed Sacrament. He is further bound to reside in his diocese for a great part of the year even though he has a coadjutor bishop. The length of his holidays is determined fairly exactly (can. 338, sect. 1 and 2), and it is his normal duty to remain near the cathedral church during Advent and Lent and at Christmas, Easter, Whitsun and Corpus Christi, though a grave and urgent reason may excuse him from this duty (can. 338, sect. 3).

The bishop is bound to apply his Mass for the people of his diocese on some eighty-eight days in the year. If he is unable to celebrate the Mass himself, he may designate some other priest for the purpose. If this is impossible on the actual feast, he should, in person or otherwise, have the Mass said as soon as may be (can. 339).

In the exercise of his pastoral care, the bishop is obliged to make a report on the state of his diocese to Rome at five-yearly intervals. A concession is made to recently appointed bishops, who, if the beginning of the year when the report falls due comes within their first two years of office, may postpone their report until the next time when it becomes obligatory (can. 340).

In connection with the report on the diocese the bishop is obliged to make a visit *ad limina* in the same year in which the report is required. For bishops whose dioceses lie within the boundaries of Europe this visit takes place every five years; for others every ten years (can. 341). This duty may be fulfilled through a coadjutor, if one is attached to the diocese, or, by special leave of the apostolic see, through some other priest who is capable of making the report and is resident within the diocese (can. 342).

Lastly, a very important duty of every diocesan bishop is to visit his diocese every year, in part or as a whole, in such a manner that he will have covered the whole diocese within a period of five years. In the United States this duty, according to the Third Council of Baltimore, should be carried out within a period of *three* years. The purpose of these pastoral visits is to "ensure the maintenance of sound and orthodox doctrine, to safeguard morality and to correct evils, to promote among clergy and people peace, innocence, piety and discipline, and to assure in general the welfare of religion" (can. 343, sect. 1). If he is unable personally to visit the whole diocese in the time allowed he may make use of a vicar-general or of some other cleric (*ibid.*). It is usual for bishops to combine these visits with the administration of confirmation in a parish, though this sacrament is also frequently bestowed outside the times of visitations.

On his visitation round the bishop may be accompanied

by two clerics as his companions and helpers who may be chosen from among the canons of the cathedral or from those of a collegiate body. The bishop's freedom of choice is emphasized, so that any privilege or custom that might limit his choice is rejected (can. 343, sect. 2).

The visit is said to be made to persons, things and holy places. The *persons* in question are, first, the clergy, especially those with the cure of souls, the faithful, and the confraternities and other bodies of the kind. The *things* include the furniture and vestments of the churches, the sacred vessels of the altar and other adjuncts of the Church's worship, and also the holy relics kept within the church and sacristy. The *holy places* mentioned are the churches and oratories (these latter being distinguished as public, semi-public and private), cemeteries, schools and all other buildings of this sort (can. 344). The spirit of the visitation is, above all, fatherly and far removed from that of an inquisitor (can. 345). If any penances are imposed for some breach of regulations they are normally very light ones. The bishop is urged to avoid all unnecessary delays, a recommendation after the manner of the Council of Trent which, in its 24th session (c. 3), says that the visits should be carried out with all necessary diligence, but "as quickly as possible" (*quam celerrime*). No gifts may be accepted, but some provisions in kind, such as board and lodging, in addition to travelling expenses, may be expected of the churches that are visited (can. 346).

THE BISHOP'S PRIVILEGES

According to canon 347 the bishop in his own diocese takes precedence of all other prelates with the exception of cardinals, papal legates, and his own archbishop. It seems clear from this canon that within his own territory he can claim precedence over patriarchs and primates. A canon is added (348) about titular bishops. They have no right of precedence in their (usually) remote dioceses, and do not take possession of their sees. It is suitable that, as an act of charity, they should from time to time celebrate Mass for their titular dioceses, but they are under no obligation to do so.

Both diocesan and titular bishops enjoy certain privileges from the moment when they receive authentic notice of their canonical institution; indeed, they have a share in some of the cardinalitial privileges enumerated in can. 239, sect. 1. So all bishops are entitled to celebrate, and cause to be celebrated in their presence, Mass on a portable altar (can. 239, sect. 1, n. 7), to celebrate Mass at sea, with all proper precautions against the possible upsetting of the chalice (n. 8); to celebrate everywhere according to the calendar of their own diocese (n. 9); to have a personal privileged altar every day (n. 10); to gain indulgences by using the prescribed prayers in their own oratories (n. 11); to bless the people solemnly (n. 12). They have further privileges as given under can. 239, sect. 1, nn. 2–6, i.e. of choosing a confessor for themselves and the members of their households (n. 2); of preaching everywhere, provided they have the permission, at least presumed, of the local ordinary (n. 3); of celebrating, or causing to be celebrated in their presence, a Mass on Maundy Thursday and the three Masses of Christmas (n. 4), provided they are not already obliged to celebrate in the cathedral; to bless and indulgence rosaries, crucifixes, and other devotional objects with a single sign of the cross (n. 5); and to bless and erect the Stations of the Cross, and also to bless crucifixes, attaching to them the indulgences of the Stations for the use of those who cannot perform the way of the Cross in the normal manner (n. 6).

In the matter of episcopal costume they are entitled to wear some items of this, such as the purple cassock and mantle, with biretta and skull-cap of the same colour, from the moment of their appointment. Other items are not to be worn before the episcopal consecration, for example, the pectoral cross and ring, the mitre, gloves, dalmatic and tunic.

From the moment of appointment they all have the right to the style *Most Reverend Excellency,* and diocesan bishops, from the time of their taking possession of their sees, have the right to receive the episcopal mensal fund, to grant indulgences of fifty days within their own territory, and to set up, in all the churches of the diocese, a throne with a canopy (can. 349, sect. 2).

RESIGNATION OF THE EPISCOPAL OFFICE

As has been said already there is no canon dealing *ex professo* with this subject. The power of order is, of course, indelible, but a bishop's jurisdiction can be removed in a variety of ways, e.g. by transfer to another see, which might be effected with or without the subject's full agreement. This method of removal occurs, very frequently, when a bishop is promoted to an archiepiscopal see. Translation from one diocese to another implies a vacancy in the original see. The bishop who is being translated is required to take possession of his new diocese within four months of receiving notice of his translation. In the meantime, he retains in his former see the position of a vicar-capitular, whose business is to maintain order and discipline in the diocese, pending the appointment of a new ordinary.

A bishop may also resign his see for reasons of health or on some other serious ground. For the validity of such a resignation the leave of the apostolic see is required. The canonists distinguish between resignation simply of the see, in which event the bishop leaves his see but retains the title and the exercise of the episcopate, whereas occasionally resignation includes not only the see but the episcopal dignity, as when a bishop decides to enter a religious order. One example of the latter could be the case of Mgr de Souza e Costa, for some years bishop of Amazoni in Brazil, who was transferred to the titular see of Tubuna when he became a Camaldolese monk at Frascati on April 12, 1914.[3]

Two other methods of creating a vacancy are mentioned by canonists under the headings of deprivations and deposition. Either of these punishments would only be inflicted in the event of some serious offence. The pope alone could pronounce sentence of this kind. No ordinary earthly ruler has any right to sever the close link between a bishop and his diocese.

[3] Cf. *Annuaire Pontifical Catholique,* 1921, pp. 374–5.

CHAPTER IV

THE SHEPHERD OF THE
LOCAL CHURCH

The bishop is a member of the episcopal body, whether in council or dispersed throughout the world; he is also head of a particular or local Church, called a diocese. We shall use this second term primarily in the familiar sense of a juridicial community of ecclesiastical origin, a defined territory placed under the authority of a bishop. First of all, we must consider the local Church in its mysterious reality. Jesus Christ founded one single Church, which was already established in the Cenacle on the day of Pentecost. The universal Church is the first Church. She it is who, through the ages, gives birth to local Churches. Each of these exists by divine right in the bishop who fathers and personifies it. In his Church, he represents Christ, the great Envoy and the true Shepherd.

CHRIST, ENVOY AND SHEPHERD

Mission means sending: a missionary is one sent, an envoy. There is only one plenary mission, the sending of the Son by the Father, of the Spirit by the Father and the Son, in the inner life of the divine Trinity. We need only quote St John, recording our Lord's words: "I do not do anything on my own authority, but speak as my Father has instructed me to speak, and he who sent me is with me: he has not left me all alone, since what I do is always what pleases him" (8. 28–9). "I will ask the Father, and he will give you another to befriend you, one who is to dwell continually with you for ever. It is the truth-giving Spirit" (14. 16–17).

On this invisible mission depends not only the visible mission of the Son in the Incarnation and of the Holy Spirit since Pentecost, but also the mission of the Church and the apostles, of the Twelve and their successors and those associated with them. "Thou hast sent me into the world on thy errand, and I have sent them into the world on my errand" (John 17. 18). It is then in the Holy Trinity that we must seek the origin of the apostolate, of mission. "Apostle" from the Greek *apostolos,* "sent out", is the same as "envoy". To be convinced of this, we have only to study the Fathers of the Church, especially St Irenaeus and St Augustine, and spiritual writers like Bérulle.

This mission is a movement, clearly indicated in the prologue to St John's Gospel, coming down from the divine Unity to universality, giving to those who have received the Word, who is true light, the power to become children of God, and made to ascend again from universality to unity, in the glory received from his Father by his only Son, full of grace and truth (John 1. 12–14). It is beyond our power to grasp the mystery. Happily our Lord reveals that he is sent by his Father as a Shepherd.

In the Old Testament the prophet Ezechiel, recording the words of the Lord, rebukes the bad shepherds who have not guarded the flock or cared for the sickly lambs or brought home the lost sheep. He proclaims: "they shall have a single shepherd to tend them now: who should tend them but my servant David? He shall be their shepherd, and I, the Lord, will be their God ... undisturbed they shall dwell in their own lands. Flock of mine, the Lord God says, flock of my pasturing ..." (Ezech. 34; cf. Zach. 13. 7, 9).

It is a foreshadowing of the parable of the lost sheep (Matt. 18. 12–14) and the Messianic prediction of the allegory of the good shepherd. These should be read again and pondered.

> The man who climbs into the sheep-fold by some other way, instead of entering by the door, comes to steal and to plunder: it is the shepherd, who tends the sheep, who comes in by the door.... Believe me, it is I who am the door of the sheep-fold.... I have come so that they may have life, and have it more abundantly. I am the good shepherd. The good shepherd lays down his life for his sheep.... My sheep are known to me, and know me, just as I am known to my Father, and know him. And for these sheep I am laying down my life. I have other sheep too, which do not belong to this fold; I must bring them in too; they will listen to my voice; so there will be one fold, and one shepherd (John 10. 1–16).

These last words reveal to us that the true Shepherd, who will sacrifice himself for his own, whom he loves to the uttermost, wishes us to be one, as he is one with the Father in the unity of the Holy Spirit. "I am not asking that thou shouldst take them out of the world, but that thou shouldst keep them clear of what is evil.... It is not only for them that I pray; I pray for those who are to find faith in me through their word; that they may all be one; that they too may be one in us, as thou, Father, art in me, and I in thee; so that the world may come to believe that it is thou who hast sent me" (John 17. 15, 20, 21)

THE BISHOP AS SHEPHERD

Jesus Christ is the true shepherd and bishop of souls (1 Peter 2. 25). He lives in the pastors of his Church, the Bride of the Spirit. Listen to the most apt words of the present Pope on the day of his coronation:

> The new pontiff is still, above all, one who realizes in himself the splendid image of the good shepherd, as the evangelist St John describes him, using the very words which came from the lips of our divine Saviour: "I am the door of the sheep" (John 10. 7).
>
> Into this fold of Jesus Christ none can enter except under the guidance of the Sovereign Pontiff, and men cannot find salvation unless they are united to him, for the Roman Pontiff is the vicar of Jesus Christ and represents him on earth.... What we have most at heart is our charge as shepherd of the whole flock... and the central point is the zeal of the good shepherd, ready for all holy daring, upright, faithful even to the supreme sacrifice. The good shepherd lays down his life for the sheep (John 10. 11), and they all follow him. If need be, he fights against the wolf to protect them.
>
> Then the horizon widens: "I have other sheep, too, which do not belong to this fold; I must bring them in too; they will listen to my voice; so there will be one fold, and one shepherd" (John 10. 16). There we have the missionary problem in all its breadth! (*Homily to the bishops and faithful present at his coronation*, November 4th, 1958).

Within due proportion, every bishop can apply this declaration to himself. He is above all the shepherd of the flock committed to him. And as the sheep and the lambs need to live, to be fed and to grow up shielded from dangers, so the pastor will have to teach as doctor, to convey life through the sacraments and the eucharistic sacrifice, and to exercise governing authority. He has the right and the duty to rule his Church in both spiritual and temporal matters with legislative, judicial and coercive power, exercised according to the holy canons (can. 335, par. 1). He is the steward of Christ, charged with giving the whole household its allowance of food (Luke 12. 42–8).

The three great prerogatives—the teaching office, the priesthood and government—derive from the sacred mission of representing the divine shepherd. The power of jurisdiction is normally the emanation of the power of Order, bestowed at the episcopal consecration.

In the words of Dom Gréa, "the bishop's mission and his priesthood are in fact simply a consequence and a communication of the mission and priesthood of Jesus Christ, and we find in him all the properties of this august and primary government" (*L'Église et sa divine constitution*).

Our Lord has defined the apostolic task which has to be continued: "Go out and make disciples . . . baptize them". Does this not assign to the successors of the apostles the prerogative and the obligation of following him as the *way* (or the shepherd), as the *truth* (or the teacher), as the *life* (or the father)?

Euntes: Go out, poor men of Galilee or other lands, not only within the confines of your native land, privileged as it may be by the covenant made with your fathers. Go into all the known world, go to the ends of the earth. Chosen by Christ (acting through the medium of the pope), speak to all generations, all peoples, all classes. Care for the faithful, of course, for those who already believe, but need to receive without too much difficulty the sacraments of penance and the Eucharist, to have their charity enlarged, to cause justice to prevail. Go to seek out the lost sheep, the fallen wayfarer, imitating the good shepherd and the good Samaritan.

Some rural regions are becoming depopulated, to the advantage of the towns, whose suburbs are growing to alarming proportions. Go, then, zealous priests, fellow-workers of your bishop, grouped in teams of priests, to the country and among the urban masses. The members of the diocesan *corps*, united to their head and to one another, are all at the service of souls.

The missionary spirit should affect the seminarists, offering their prayers and their long and arduous studies for the evangelization of the parishes and the diocese, who surround them with such confident affection. The religious, both men and women, are privileged auxiliaries of those who have the cure of souls. What help the cloisters give in fertilizing difficult harvest-fields!

Lay Christians, too, go forth in the name of Christ and the Church, to the hard toil of evangelization, in the parish and your places of work, in the industrial areas and the suburbs. Like the present Pope and his predecessor, your bishop counts on you. Do not forget your duties in the temporal sphere, applying Christian social teaching. Some will not have the time or the aptitude, being prevented from working for spiritual revival or the transformation of the social system. Let them pray and dedicate themselves, accomplishing such apostolate as they can. But they must be careful not to plunge into new movements which are not approved by the head of the diocese. Some may be satisfied with merely being associated with those excellent pious groups, like the "Apostleship of Prayer", while they ought to be actively working under their parish priest, according to the directions of their bishop.

The testimony of a genuine Catholicism, without partiality or self-seeking, will have its effect on the mass of those who are far from the flock. The bishop himself carries his crozier, not as a sceptre of domination, but as a shepherd's crook. His duty is to guide into the true pastures those for whom he is responsible in the sight of God. He will be in closer and more frequent touch with his priests, since he must really be, like the pope, the "servant of the servants of God". He will guide and encourage them in their noble and difficult task. What joy it is for him and for them when young men come forward in their turn for the conquest of souls!

How many homes would be more united and set a better example if there had been more care for the guidance of engaged couples, more preparation for marriage! Let us congratulate the movements that have already begun to bear fruit, and extend the influence of their meetings. Let us remind men of the rights of the family, and the duties it demands. Family associations have surely the opportunity and the duty to defend public morality, by getting a ban imposed on suggestive advertisements, indecent films and degrading amusements.

New forms of apostolate, regional missions, research in religious sociology, are springing up nearly everywhere. There are those, behind their times, who will complain that this is all new-fangled. The bishops, priests and laity who came before us no doubt did what they could and ought. They are now in heaven or purgatory. But nowadays coordinated pastoral work is a general duty. Work in common, according to clearcut views, will enable us to act with more infectious joy and success. Behind these researches we must see souls to be better known, to be approached, defended from false shepherds, warned against the propagandists of the sects, pushing into their houses. More than our forebears, in these difficult times, we can depend on an *élite* among the laity. "The laity are posted in the front lines of the life of the Church.... They in consequence, they above all," said Pius XII, "should be ever more clearly conscious that they not only belong to the Church but *are* the Church, that is, the community of the faithful on earth, under the leadership of a common head, the pope, and the bishops in communion with him" (Allocution, February 18th, 1946).

Let us urge them to be for their milieu, for their parish, for the young, true worshippers of the Father, marching hand in hand, in this age of technical progress, towards the light. The cross, which the bishop wears on his breast and signs before his name, should be the rallying-standard which will bring victory.

THE BISHOP AS TEACHER

Go out: yes, but also teach, so that the truth of the Gospel may remain in our possession (Gal. 2. 5). There is only one Truth, for there is but one God, the God of science and of faith. The bishop has the duty of guarding the faith and handing it on.

Preaching first by his example, he must preach by personal teaching in his sermons and exhortations in ever changing circumstances, instruct and stimulate by pastoral letters, communications and directions. His duty is imperative: to watch over the regular and satisfying preaching of his priests and the orthodoxy of clerical studies. Our Lord said to his disciples: "You are the salt of the earth, the light of the world" (Matt. 5. 13, 14). It is to reveal the true face of Christianity to the indifferent and to adversaries who may well be sincere, to those who might become ardent apostles like Paul of Tarsus, to give warnings against distortions and harmful reading. That is why the faithful are forbidden to publish books on religion without the bishop's *imprimatur*. His duty is to understand how to support the press, the journals and reviews which spread the truth, to publish abroad the truth "on the housetops" by radio and television, but also to speak out fearlessly in condemnation when some falsehood is spread, when Catholic unity is attacked, when some scandal is about to contaminate the flock.

The diocesan synod, held at least every ten years, is a more solemn occasion for codifying the statutes of local law. The bishop is the sole legislator, after he has taken the considered advice of the dignitaries and the delegates of the clergy.

In 1961 the present pope held the most recent of the synods of Rome. Two of these took place after the return of the popes from Avignon, and the last in 1461 under Pius II.

As fatherly upholder of discipline, for which he must render an account to the Holy See every five years, the bishop is the judge of faith, fulfilling the ministry of the prophets and teachers (*Didache,* 15, 6). He must preach in season and, if need be, out of season (2 Tim. 4. 2). His remote predecessors, whose tombs have become glorious cathedrals, were the defenders of the city. The bishop always holds the power of the Magisterium, not to enforce his own opinions and show off his culture, but to "guard the deposit" as dispenser of the word of truth, according to Scripture and tradition (1 Tim. 6. 20).

THE BISHOP AS FATHER, CONVEYING SUPERNATURAL LIFE

"I have come so that they may have life, and have it more abundantly" (John 10. 10). The bishop, spouse of his Church (as symbolized by his pastoral ring), is the father of souls, charged to communicate to them life and grace through the sacraments, of which he is the chief minister. He is the *summus sacerdos,* the high priest, to whom belongs the right of conferring baptism, as Tertullian states (*De Baptismate,* c. XVII). To him is reserved, in principle, the right to baptize adults. He administers confirmation, except to the dying, for whom the parish priest can take his place. He calls men to the ministry and confers holy Orders on them. Without a bishop there would be no priesthood. What supernatural joy it is for him when he engenders priests, to be, like him, "stewards of God's mysteries" (1 Cor. 4. 1), and especially of the Eucharist! As St Jerome says, the priest has the same power as the bishop to offer Mass validly. But the bishop's permission is necessary for it to be licit. The sacred altar-stone, the chalice and the paten must have been consecrated by him with the oils which he has the privilege of making fruitful in the ceremony of the Church's unity at the Chrismal Mass of Maundy Thursday. This Mass, now separated from the Mass of the Institution of the Eucharist, ought to be attended by all the faithful who are free, and as many religious and priests as possible. The bishop alone pronounces the consecratory words over the oils, but he is assisted by seven deacons and seven subdeacons, and by twelve priests who perform the sacred actions in silence, just as they lay their hands on new priests. These oils are used on those being baptized and confirmed, for the ordination of priests and the consecration of bishops, for those who receive Extreme Unction, and for the solemn blessing of churches and bells.

The bishop controls the power of remitting sins. His authority is needed to absolve, except in those cases where "the Church supplies". The office of official witness at a Christian marriage falls to the parish priest (as authorized by his bishop), who has the right to receive the consent of the spouses and to delegate authority for this purpose.

Grace is conveyed through the sacraments, and especially through Holy Communion, now so much easier to receive, with our evening Masses and the mitigation of the fast before Communion. Grace flows into souls through the life of private prayer and the liturgical spirit. The bishop, on the model of Christ, is the great leader and president of public worship. He has the privilege of giving the threefold blessing in the name of the Trinity, whereas the priest in his presence blesses only after bowing to him.

In the first ages of the Church, there was only the one Mass of the bishop, assisted by the priests and deacons. Even when there were "titular" or daughter churches of the cathedral, in which the bishop's throne was set up, the clergy of the episcopal city took part in the sacred functions as regularly as they could. Even in our days, canon law leaves it to the bishop to fix the hours of the public services, and that for several reasons, one of which is to make sure that the bishop will be attended by a representative number of priests and people. The pontifical Mass in all its splendour is the only Mass which fully teaches the lessons of unity, the return to the sources, called for by attachment to the diocesan Church and, through it, to the Church universal. We no longer send a portion of the Host consecrated by the bishop to be placed in the chalice at other Masses, as a mark of unity. But the names of the chief pastors, the pope and the diocesan bishop, uttered at every Mass, remind us that if the Catholic Church is to be at peace, protected, united and governed, she must be in union with the successors of Peter and the apostles (Canon of the Mass, *pacificare, custodire, adunare et regere*).

According to St Ignatius of Antioch, a Church is essentially a unity grouped around a single bishop. The spiritual unity of souls with Christ is dependent on their visible union with his representative, the bishop. In his eyes, there is but one God, one Christ, one faith, one bishop. "Do nothing without the bishop in what concerns the Church. Perform all your actions in that spirit of concord which pleases God, under the presidency of the bishop, who holds the place of God" (*Smyrn.* 1, 2). "I congratulate you, Church of Ephesus, that you are united to your bishop as the Church is to Jesus Christ, and as Jesus Christ is to his Father, that the whole may be in unity" (*Ephes.* 5). The same doctrine is professed by St Irenaeus, who had come from Asia to Lyons, recognizing in "the Elder" the man who embodies tradition.

The successor of the apostles may never lose sight of his charge: to edify, to build up, to strengthen the whole Church, as a pillar in part supports the building, contributing to its strength and harmony. Handing on to his clergy and people the teachings of Catholic doctrine, the laws of morality and the measures necessary for general order, providing them with supernatural life, the bishop is the centre of unity.

CHAPTER V

THE BISHOP AND THE PRIESTS

Till the end of time our Lord will have men who perpetuate his priesthood. Some, the bishops, will do so in the fullest degree possible; others, plain priests, though not possessing all the prerogatives of the bishops, have the honour and the duty of sharing in the priestly powers of Christ. As Pius XII emphasized in his discourse to the cardinals and bishops taking part in the solemnity of "Mary, Queen of Heaven and Earth" (*A.A.S.*, Nov. 28th, 1954), the peculiar and principal function of the priest is, and has always been, to "sacrifice". To offer the sacrifice of the Mass belongs only to the celebrant, who occupies the place of Jesus Christ. What an honour, and what a mark of confidence! What a privilege, not shared by the laity! The laity have, indeed, in a very true sense, that "royal priesthood" of which we read in I Peter (2. 9), enabling them to take part in the eucharistic sacrifice and to offer up their bodies as a living sacrifice, holy and acceptable to God (Rom. 12. 1). But they do not share in the sacerdotal power. Great is the dignity of priests. It must be honoured by all. The bishop, the chief representative of the Saviour in his Church, is more specially endued with it. It is with pride and emotions that he sings, at the end of the ordination of priests, "I will not call you servants, but my friends".

THE PRIEST, THE BISHOP'S HELPER
AS SHEPHERD

The offering of the holy sacrifice of the Mass requires numerous priests able to effect our Lord's presence on the altars of our churches and chapels, and equally the pastoral mission entrusted to the head of a diocese can only be carried out with the cooperation of his sons in the priesthood. How could any bishop single-handed administer the sacraments, teach the children, instruct the faithful, seek the wandering sheep, visit the sick and those in full health in their homes, assist the dying, conduct funerals? Without priests in the town and country parishes, the educational institutions, the centres of influence, how could he carry the Gospel into the life of the people, inspire movements of Catholic Action, apply the social doctrines of the Church? A bishop can do little without holy priests or usually, without priests well trained and in sufficient numbers. One of his first objectives will be to ensure replacements, by imparting to all around him his apostolic zeal.

UNION WITH THE BISHOP IS NECESSARY
TO THE PRIEST

However meritorious the ministry of the priest may be, it will be barren if he cannot count on the support of his bishop. It is to a successor of the apostles that he owes his priestly character. To be a true minister of Christ and his Church, he must remain in communion with the ecclesiastical hierarchy; with the pope, the immediate pastor of all the sheep and lambs of the divine flock; with the bishop, guide and guardian of the diocesan flock, and above all of its chosen members, the priests. A clergy which lost contact with the teaching Church and its paternal government would endanger both its faith and its loyalty. Error and laxity would spread. Every one would be blown about at the mercy of differing opinions, unprotected from bad examples. God has instituted pastors, not in order to impose an additional burden, but to transmit life and to propagate it more abundantly in their flocks, whom they have to cause to grow in an ever closer imitation of Christ. When bishops and priests can speak to each other with confidence, understand and supplement each other, then there is mutual security and each supports the other.

A bishop is happy when his priests are happy. He suffers with them, sometimes through them. He rejoices in their joys, offering his life for those who are so closely associated with him, and whose merits and virtues are the finest jewels in his episcopal crown.

THE BISHOP, PRINCIPLE OF PERFECTION FOR HIS PRIESTS

The Church needs priests who are not only upright but striving after perfection. "Lord, give us holy priests", is the heartfelt prayer of our congregations. One holy priest does more good than a dozen others who are more like painstaking officials. The Curé d'Ars is a model who has his imitators in the ranks of our diocesan priests, at all levels. The secular clergy has had its saints, and not only in those early ages when almost all the founders of Churches were canonized by the voice of the faithful. In the last twelve centuries, more than 380 of its members have been raised to the altars, and about 265 of them were neither bishops nor religious: eleven were canonized and nine beatified as confessors, five were canonized and 240 beatified as martyrs. Mgr Charue, Bishop of Namur, who publishes this glorious roll of honour in his book *Le Clergé diocésain,* specifies that these include about ten vicars-general, about seventy-five rectors and thirty-five curates, some thirty professors, including about ten in the seminaries, and a number of missionaries. This list of priestly saints will of course be increased by the canonization causes now being considered.

Hence we cannot accept the idea that what we call the secular clergy is of a second grade, or of less value than the regular clergy. It must be clearly asserted that there is only one priesthood, being sanctified by fidelity to the chosen vocation, to the graces so profusely lavished by our Lord on his elect who remain united to the hierarchy he has established. The religious find the source of their sanctity in their direct dependence on the pope. The priests incardinated in a diocese have to be sanctified with the help of their father and pontiff, the diocesan bishop.

The term "secular clergy", used in canon law, seems to many to have an unfavourable sense, as if those who belong to it were less regular, perhaps because of their life in the midst of the world. On the contrary, it means that according to the will of our Lord (John 17. 15), the apostles must remain in the midst of the life of the world. If some prefer the term "diocesan clergy", it is certainly with no idea of excluding the religious from the life of the diocese, but in order to make it clearer that one can strive for perfection in the magnificent state of a priest consecrated to God by the sacramental character of Order, working in the service of the souls of a diocese, under the direct guidance of the bishop.

The first priests, members of the *presbyterium*, entrusted themselves to the guidance of those who had succeeded the apostles. Our priests today can find all the means of sanctification by fulfilling their task in the clergy of the local Church to which they belong.

The bishop is dedicated to a state of perfection, for he dedicates himself definitively to the service of God, in the persons of all those whom he has to sanctify. Is this not a self-subjection as complete as that of a religious? The religious dedicates himself to seek perfection: he is not expected to *be* perfect. In the bishop, on the contrary, perfection is presumed. The sanctity he has to communicate to others he must possess himself.... Devotedness to others takes for granted in pastors an abounding charity which deprives itself of the sweetness of contemplation and generously engages in the conquest of souls, to win them to him whom it loves above all (Dom Lottin, "La doctrine de Saint Thomas sur l'état religieux", in *La Vie Spirituelle*, 1923, pp. 391–2).

"Ordination is not merely a transmission of juridical and liturgical powers; it is a sacramental act which confers a grace of sanctity" (Dom Botte, *L'Ordre d'après les prières d'ordination*). It is participation in the priestly charisma.

Now, the priest lawfully ordained, a pastor under the bishop's authority, must share in the bishop's responsibilities becoming all things to all men, wherever he is sent by the obedience he promised on the day of his ordination. The father does not only give life, he must sustain it by his example and advice, by retreats, days of recollection and priestly gatherings. The bishop is the embodiment of the "duty of state" as the source of holiness. The priest too will sanctify himself in his ministry, going to the utmost limits of the duty of his state. Though he is not canonically established in a state of perfection, yet being associated with his bishop in union with the pope, he must strive to make himself ever nearer to the only real Priest, the one True, the one Holy: *Tu solus sanctus.*

Hence, in the practice of holy continence and of sometimes heroic obedience, in detachment from worldly goods and often in real poverty, the priest in the service of souls progresses towards holiness. This is "the charity which is the bond of perfection".

We are far from denying the benefit of priestly societies of perfection. The Society of the Priests of St Francis de Sales, the Apostolic Union, the secular institutes, like that of the Priests of the Heart of Jesus, the Prado, the Third Orders, the Fraternities of Charles de Foucauld, the Association of Priests-Adorers, attachment to an abbey as Oblates, etc., all these do splendid work. These bodies cannot possibly become a barrier between the diocesan priest and his bishop. The bishop has the grace of state to promote the sanctity of the "cooperators in his order", providing them with the means to sanctify themselves by doing good, to fight against isolation and too great emphasis on external activity, in fidelity to prayer and the devotional exercises prescribed by canon law and the diocesan statutes, in a spirit of ecclesiastical brotherhood and filial trust, proud of accomplishing the important task of a priest who works lovingly for the glory of God and the salvation of souls.

BENEFITS TO BE EXPECTED FROM COORDINATED PASTORAL WORK UNDER THE BISHOP

The diocese is a family. This family spirit has always been the mark of the diocesan clergy, even when communications were more difficult. One was proud to belong to the clergy of some large diocese—mentioning it with pardonable vanity—of a Christian diocese, with gratitude to one's predecessors, especially if it has the apostolic ardour to help a poorer diocese; of a poorer, more austere, diocese, for often trouble or trial increases intimacy and makes one less selfish. We must realize that today contacts are more frequent, relations between colleagues easier. Then the progress of Catholic Action, both general and specialized, on the one hand, and the more or less general dechristianization on the other, make genuine collaboration necessary. Evil is so deep-seated that individual conversion, essential as it is, is no longer sufficient. Pius XII exhorted the bishops of France "to arouse among the faithful under their charge a *collective effort* for the Christian renewal of society" (Encyclical on the first centenary of the Appearances at Lourdes, July 2nd, 1957). This is even truer for the priests, certainly on the natural level, but above all on the diocesan.

Sociological research and inquiries into religious practice have brought parish priests and their parishioners closer together, but also, and more important, they have brought the priests together under the guidance of their bishop. On the pastoral committees there are parish priests, chaplains of Catholic Action, schools and hospitals, teachers, and religious. They inform and instruct one another, and act in concert, under the direction of one of the bishop's representatives, and often of the bishop himself.

How important it is that everyone should look beyond the horizon of his parochial or scholastic cares and bear his part in the responsibilities of the diocese! It is even more essential to the onward progress of the Church, and more edifying in every sense, that priests should not look on their bishop merely as their administrator and chief.

Many grave and difficult problems will thus find a more human and positive solution. The father listens patiently to the confidences of his sons in the priesthood; for is he not the bond of union, and above all individualism and factions?

The diocesan clergy, understanding how essential they are, will be encouraged to follow out their mission. Disregarding the critics who would spread defeatism and give bad impressions, let us take a broad view, looking to the ends of the inhabited world, using the stepping-stones we have, let us build up and extend the Church in this springtime, the hour of the Council which aspires to unity.

CHAPTER VI

THE BISHOP AND THE STATES OF PERFECTION

"It is God's will that all should be saved" (1 Tim. 2. 4). To all alike our Lord says: "Be perfect, as your Father in heaven is perfect." The episcopate supposes an obligation to the perfect practice of charity in the perpetual care of souls.

As the husband must leave everything for his wife, so the bishop no longer belongs to himself, he must give himself up entirely to his Church. Since the coming of the Gospel, the exercise of authority has been a service, a sort of slavery. "What is the episcopate," says Bossuet, "but a state of servitude, imposed on us by charity for the saving of souls?" There is nothing more formidable, nothing more exacting, but nothing is more detaching, more gladdening. Jesus told Peter that to have the charge of souls means to love more (Cardinal Richaud, funeral oration on Cardinal Saliège).

THE BISHOP IN A STATE OF PERFECTION

St Paul's pastoral epistles sum up the virtues befitting those who have received the grace of the priesthood by the "laying on of hands", both bishops and presbyters, without distinction of degree. These counsels may then be addressed to all priests, but they certainly concern bishops, for tradition agrees that that is what Timothy and Titus were. "The man who is to be a bishop must be one in whom no fault can be found; faithful to one wife, sober, discreet, modest, well-behaved, hospitable, experienced in teaching, no lover of wine or of brawling, courteous, neither quarrelsome nor grasping. . . . Make thyself a model of speech and behaviour for the flock, all faith, all love, all purity" (1 Tim. 3. 2–7; 4. 12). The apostle requires the bishop to have been only once married: even among the schismatics he is bound to perfect chastity, so as to be wholly devoted to his chaste spouse, the Church. He must suffer for her, devote himself to piety and preach a doctrine consistent with it. He is positively bound to holiness by his consecration, which makes him both the high priest and the good shepherd of his diocese.

BISHOPS AMONG THE SAINTS

If it is unhappily true that there have been mediocre and bad bishops, a very great number have set an example of the highest virtues. The canonization causes of several bishops are at this moment being considered. The names of former pastors, defenders of the city, are found on almost every page of the Martyrology. Among the best known since the sixteenth century we may cite St John Fisher, cardinal, bishop of Rochester, and martyr (1535); St Charles Borromeo, cardinal and archbishop of Milan (1584); St Francis de Sales, bishop of Geneva and doctor of the Church (1622); St Gregory Barbarico, bishop of Bergamo and Padua (1697); St Alphonsus Liguori, founder of the Redemptorists, bishop of St Agatha and doctor of the Church (1787); St Anthony Mary Claret, founder of the Claretians, archbishop of Santiago in Cuba (1870); St Pius X, former curate and rector, principal of a seminary and chancellor, bishop of Mantua, patriarch of Venice, pope (1914). And there are also many beatified.

THE BISHOP AND THE RELIGIOUS COMMUNITIES

The bishop, "as the perfecter", is in a state of perfection, perfection acquired and to be communicated. St Thomas states that he exercises the *magisterium* of perfection, and consequently the religious state pertains to the episcopal state, as the action of teaching pertains to the teaching office: *sicut disciplina ad magisterium* (*Summa Theol.*, IIa–IIae, qu. 185, art. 8).

Far, then, from being opposed to the religious life, the bishop has the duty to favour and protect it and the other forms of states of perfection. On June 16th, 628, the abbot of the famous monastery of Bobbio received from Pope Honorius a Bull withdrawing him from all but papal jurisdiction, and since then, no doubt, the religious orders (and to some extent other institutes also) have been exempted in various ways from the authority of the local bishop. The question is always liable to be reopened. The present writer, being a member of the Commission on Religious in preparation for the Second Vatican Council, is specially bound to discretion.

On April 12th, 1961, the Pope presided over a study session of this Commission, during which he delivered an allocution, which was thus reported in the *Osservatore Romano* of April 13th:

The Holy Father, speaking in Latin, had words of sympathy and encouragement for all, and developed three special points. He emphasized first the need for greater coordination of all the magnificent energies of the religious in the works of the apostolate, under the wise guidance of the bishops. He further recommended the exercise of the fundamental virtues proper to those who have consecrated their whole lives to the Lord, without which virtues these works could not bear abundant fruit for good. Finally, His Holiness urged that particular stress be laid on obedience, which is the guarantee of success, and ensures the avoidance of those singularities in the work of the ministry that might have pernicious results.

The enclosed monasteries of men and women have their vocation of contemplation and penance to follow; dedicated primarily to divine worship, they draw down the protection of heaven on the Church militant. Then the pope must have "shock troops" at his disposal for the apostolate, especially in the missions. The religious communities, particularly of clerics, which extend beyond the bounds of a diocese, are under the direct authority of the pope for their internal government, with adaptations necessary for their own activities, and in accordance with the spirit of each congregation.

It is important to preserve a basic uniformity of rules, constitutions and directories of the institutes of pontifical status, and even of those of diocesan status when they extend beyond the area of a diocese.

The Ordinary of a mother-house should not keep the nuns too exclusively for the works of his fold when they might be more useful elsewhere. Though the bishop is the ecclesiastical superior, he is never in the strict sense the religious superior of any congregation, even if he has used the power granted him by canon law (can. 492, par. 1) to found one, with the authorization of the Holy See. Until the papal approval, or a "decree of praise" has been obtained, the congregation remains fully subject to the jurisdiction of its various Ordinaries. No religious house may be established or suppressed in a diocese without the permission of the diocesan bishop.

The Holy Father himself is the supreme superior of all religious institutes, whose members owe him obedience in virtue of their vow. In face of modern demands and the scarcity of missionary workers, the popes are increasingly requiring the religious to take an active part in the apostolate.

This is certainly true, in the first place, of the priests. Religious and secular priests form a single whole—the diocesan clergy, under the paternal oversight of the bishop, according to the instruction of the present pope (Address to Provincial Superiors, November 13th, 1960). On the pastoral committees, the religious will usefully be given a place, corresponding to their activities on the diocesan level, just as, on the regional and national levels, periodical communications are exchanged between the representatives of the bishops and the delegates of the major superiors, including the teaching brothers.

The establishment of the diocesan sections of the three groups of sisters—parochial school-teachers, secondary school-mistresses and nurses—is full of promise and should render valuable service. The women's communities, always so glad to welcome the bishop and have contacts with him, will become more and more valuable auxiliaries of his apostolate. May they learn, under his direction, thoroughly to coordinate their efforts, being ready to abandon a house or an activity if it is already well provided for by another Congregation. They must eliminate overlapping and waste of energy and employ themselves more effectively elsewhere. Who can better guide them than the father of all concerned?

THE BISHOP AND THE SECULAR INSTITUTES

The Church adapts herself to the needs of the times. Alongside the traditional forms, new institutes have come into being, composed of clergy or laity, practising the evangelical counsels in the world. They aim at Christian perfection, working at the apostolate as seculars. Their charter is the Constitution *Provida Mater Ecclesia* of Pius XII (*A.A.S.*, 1947, p. 118), supplemented by the *Motu Proprio, Primo feliciter elapso* (*A.A.S.*, 1948, p. 285).

Many benefits may be expected from them, bringing supernatural light into worlds which are hard to penetrate, such as those of organized labour and the closed professions. Layfolk consecrated to God, respecting everyone's liberty, they work by what they are and their manner of life, slowly perhaps, but with full knowledge of their ground, to prepare it for spiritual harvests. The bishop, responsible for all who form part of his diocese, will discreetly give local directions, without losing sight of wider horizons.

These secular institutes require a specially adapted preparation. They do not make the religious congregations redundant, but they have their own providential rôle, under the inspiration of the Holy Spirit.

OTHER SOCIETIES FOR PERFECTION

With or without private vows, there are many Christian men and women who want to live in a spirit of apostolate, drawn from a deep interior life. They try to live according to the perfection of their state, and contribute their support to the apostolic work of the Church, in union with their bishops. The *Auxiliaries of the Apostolate* place themselves fully at their bishops' disposal.

We may also mention, among others, the "Sons and Daughters of St Francis de Sales", many of whom are married persons. In a rule which is both firm and flexible, and in progressive spiritual direction, they find a means of sanctifying themselves through the duties of their state and their readiness to supply the needs of their brethren. They form precious reserves of devotion, which need to be guided by the bishop, responsible as he is for the salvation of so many thousands of souls.

CHAPTER VII

THE BISHOP AND THE LAITY

The Church is composed not only of clergy and religious: the laity too are part of it. In the telling words of Pius XII, they too *are* the Church. The "holy people" (from the Greek *laos*), forming part of the flock of Christ, are entrusted to the charge of the pastor.

THE BISHOP AND THE YOUNG

The young are the hope of the flock. The bishop will give particular attention to their care. One of his first duties will be, not only to hand on to them the truth, to compose and authorize the catechism which summarizes it, but to see that Christian doctrine is communicated with every possible safeguard to the children and young people who are continuing their studies or professional training. There are institutes, reviews and catechists' meetings which help to refresh our methods in conformity with the demands of the faith. It is for the bishop to control, supervise and support all these activities.

There must be instruction and also formation for the Christian life. This is the rôle of the Catholic schools, colleges and universities. In the State institutions, the chaplains have a ministry of the highest importance. Parents have the grave duty of claiming religious instruction for their sons and daughters. The function of the bishop is to establish a diocesan catechistic office, to regulate the whole organization of the parochial catechisms and the courses appropriate to the different stages of secular instruction. He lends his authority and protection to Catholic youth organizations, holiday camps, the Cubs and Brownies, Scouts and Guides, etc., and to pious associations like the Eucharistic Crusade. "Sow hosts and you will reap priests."

THE BISHOP AND THE SEMINARIES

Among all those who will have a decisive influence on the world of tomorrow, the future priests have a very special place. They have it, be sure, in the heart of the bishop. "The hope of the harvest is in the sowing." God scatters the seed abroad according to the needs of souls. Yet "the harvest is plentiful enough, but the labourers are few" (Matt. 9. 37; Luke 10. 2).

All kinds of schools ought to provide candidates for the priesthood, but these are also found among those who are already engaged in some other profession. All the same, the junior seminaries are the houses where the appeal will be best studied and most easily followed. May good homes, stronger and more radiant, become the nurseries in which the tender plant of vocation, whether early or late, may flower!

The bishop will choose from his priests those who have the delicate mission of being spiritual directors or professors in the seminaries. The junior seminaries, where final decisions are not yet made, correspond to the education provided in Grammar Schools. The major seminary, established according to rules fixed by the Holy See and the head of the diocese, provides for the direct training of the priest, from the spiritual and pastoral point of view, and for the acquisition of sacred learning. The bishop's conscience is specially bound to this work. The future of his diocese depends on it in the highest degree. In our days, one seminary sometimes accepts the seminarists of several dioceses.

THE BISHOP AND THE APOSTOLATE OF THE LAITY

The laity have always performed some kind of apostolate. We read in St Paul's epistles that men and women collaborated with him in the propagation of the Gospel. All Christians, by the fact of their baptism, must be apostles. To carry out this mission in an individual capacity the laity need not wait for a delegation of powers: they have only to be faithful to the requirements of their state as baptized and confirmed Christians. Pius XII often referred to it, especially in his addresses to two World Congresses of the Apostolate of the Laity, on October 14th, 1951, and October 5th, 1957. "The dependence of the laity on the hierarchy admits of degrees. It is strictest for Catholic Action: this in fact represents the official apostolate of the laity."

Though not itself a "hierarchical apostolate", Catholic Action is carried on by the hierarchy's mandate. The laity, of course, cannot be fully associated with the forms of teaching, sanctification and government that belong to the bishop, but they are invited to collaborate with his apostolate of devotedness, acting on groups of men. The chaplains who train them spiritually must allow the militants real freedom of action. This is true, both for those who form part of general Catholic Action, aimed at making parishes more open-minded and missionary, and for specialized Catholic Action, evangelizing the various classes: independent, working-class and rural.

On February 5th, 1961, Cardinal Montini made a remarkable statement on the rôle of Catholic Action in the world:

> Catholic Action, by its attachment to the Church's hierarchy, realizes in the laity, at the highest point, that "royal priesthood" which is the privilege of every Christian, but in Catholic Action is taken into consideration and exercised with a clear intention.... It draws the clergy out of its isolation and calls back the people from its dispersion. From the source of the teaching Church, from its authority and grace, it draws treasures of truth, programmes of action, impulses of spirituality, and spreads them abroad among the Christian community.

THE BISHOP'S MISSION TOWARDS THE LAITY

Rich and poor, employers and employed, refugees and emigrants, all have a right to the bishop's care. Owing allegiance to no party, the pastors of souls will favour only the weak, the sick and the unfortunate. But how can they act fruitfully without the help of the laity? Their interest is indispensable if the apostolate, based on an accurate knowledge of men and their different categories, is to affect the complex of society. Would that a larger number of sincere believers might *engage* in Catholic Action, in an association of the apostolate, or of piety, of charity, such as Catholic Aid or the Brothers of St Vincent de Paul, a trade union, a family association, or a press committee!

The bishops, while allowing every man his responsibility in matters where opinion is free, have a duty to prevent wastage of man-power and to coordinate the apostolic efforts of their people.

THE BISHOP AND NON-CATHOLICS

It is the bishop's duty to be interested in the missionary apostolate. Out of some 2,700 million souls in the world, only about thirty-five per cent know Christ and seventeen per cent (about 500 millions) are Catholics. The sheep must be brought into the one true fold. It is to be hoped that the approaching Council may prepare a way for the union of those who have been separated for centuries. The bishop is responsible for making contacts with separated Christians.

Others, even many who have been baptized into the Catholic religion, are in practice far from Christ and his Church. The pastor of the diocese has many opportunities for meeting the authorities, and persons of considerable influence. How should he not be concerned for these masses who live far from God? "I have other sheep too, which do not belong to this fold." His heart, the heart of an apostle, will take every opportunity to draw them nearer to the Lord, by discreet words and unselfish acts of charity. "He must bear a good character, too, in the world's eyes" (1 Tim. 3. 7).

CHAPTER VIII

THE BISHOP AND HIS DIOCESE

The bishop, as we have seen, is teacher, high priest and pastor. If he is not principally an administrator, he has to be one, nonetheless, as the prelate appointed to govern a diocese. According to canon 329 of the code of canon law, the bishops, as successors of the apostles, are placed by divine appointment at the head of local Churches, which they rule with ordinary jurisdiction, under the authority of the pope. They are certainly not mere representatives of the pope. That is the rôle of the apostolic nuncios or internuncios, who are his ambassadors to the civil powers in each country, and of the apostolic delegates, who have no direct diplomatic functions. But a member of the episcopal college (a necessary constituent of the Church founded by our Lord), once he has been chosen by Christ's vicar, the successor of Peter, is truly the head of the diocese whose title he bears. He signs his acts and orders with his Christian name, following it with the name of the local Church, of which he is really the mystical spouse, sharing in the royal power of Christ. It is in Christ's name that he wields authority in the spiritual domain, and even in the material things which depend on it. Sometimes he has other episcopal titles as well. Some

ancient archbishoprics having been suppressed, it is the
archbishop of the ecclesiastical province who now perpetuates their former glory.

The metropolitan of Lyons, for example, primate of
the Gauls (an honorific title), is also archbishop of Vienne
in the suffragan diocese of Grenoble; that of Aix-en-
Provence is archbishop of Embrun in the territory of Gap;
that of Toulouse, of Narbonne in the circumscription of
Carcassonne. There are also ancient bishoprics within the
area of an existing diocese, which are revived with the
authorization of the Holy See. The archbishop of Avignon
has more titles than any other in France: he is bishop
of Apt, Carpentras, Cavaillon, Orange and Vaison-la-
Romaine. Next in order is the bishop of Montpellier. Many
other bishops represent famous Churches of old; Constan-
tine, for example, standing for Hippo, made illustrious
by St Augustine. The essence of any local Church is something of divine right, but its existence is not. Then a
Church can give birth to daughter Churches, as Westminster to Brentwood, Southwark to Portsmouth, Glasgow
to Motherwell and Paisley.

Only the universal Church is immortal, making good
her losses by new acquisitions, dioceses being continually
formed in lands where the faith has penetrated further or
the hierarchy has been established as in England and Scotland, the Philippines, India, China and Japan, Africa, Viet-
nam, etc. Local Churches, in Dom Gréa's picturesque
comparison, are like clusters of grapes, which have no
further reason for existence once they have produced all
their fruit. This is what has happened with dioceses whose
names are preserved in memory of their past.

If dioceses are too big they are beyond human capacity
to manage and make complete apostolic permeation impossible. At the same time it is important that the bishop

should not be responsible for too small a Church. As early as the Council of Sardica it was decreed: "It is not permitted to ordain bishops in the villages and small towns where a priest is sufficient, and the establishment of a bishop is not necessary, so that the name and authority of the episcopate may not be cheapened." For this reason some dioceses are united *ad personam*, in the person of one and the same bishop, as sometimes happens in Italy. In certain circumstances the Holy See may commit the administration of a vacant diocese either to the metropolitan or to a neighbouring bishop. This is provided for by canon law (unless specially prescribed otherwise), when a resident bishop is preferred, or transferred to another see. On the other hand, it is the cathedral chapter which must elect a vicar capitular. This official, though he cannot make innovations while the see is vacant, wields an interim authority, so that the life of the diocese may go on.

THE DIOCESE IN HISTORY

The word "diocese" is not of ecclesiastical origin, and has not always had the precise sense of the territorial area in which a bishop has "ordinary" jurisdiction, that is, in virtue of his charge. Etymologically speaking, *dioecesis* means "habitation apart", and in a derived sense a separated territory over which the particular power of an administrator was exercised. With the Greeks it was the financial or some other administration which was indicated by this term. Cicero uses it to denote a mere department of the annexes attached to a province (*Epist. ad familiares*, 13, Epist. 53, Epist. 67). From the time of Diocletian the "diocese" is no longer a subdivision of a province, but included several provinces. In the fourth century Gaul formed two dioceses, *dioecesis Galliarum*, which included the two Germanies, and *dioecesis Viennensis,* including at first five, then seven provinces, when Aquitaine and the Narbonnaise were divided: later Gaul formed only one diocese.

The first juridical text to speak of it from the point of view of the Church is the thirteenth law of the Theodosian Code. It occurs in the second canon of the Second Ecumenical Council of Constantinople and the third canon of the Council of Chalcedon, referring, however, to immense areas containing many bishoprics. It is in Africa (which constituted only one civil diocese, subdivided into six provinces) that the word is first used in the sense it has for us, in canon 92 of the Council of Carthage in 390. It was used, however, as a synonym both for "parish" and, in contrast, for an ecclesiastical province.

After the age of the itinerant bishops, the first fellow-workers and successors of the apostles, heads of geographically defined territories were appointed, often by the patriarchs and exarchs, under the influence of the Christian emperors. In 1092 Urban II wrote to Rainold, archbishop of Rheims: "It pertains only to the Apostolic See to combine or divide dioceses or to erect new ones." This is what is prescribed by the canon law still in force, in canon 215: "Only the supreme ecclesiastical authority has the power to found, modify, divide, unite or suppress ecclesiastical provinces, dioceses, abbeys and prelatures *nullius* [independent of the diocesan bishop], vicariates and prefectures apostolic" [whose holders are the pope's delegates to govern the mission, the former being in episcopal orders, whereas the latter resemble protonotaries]. Mission territories are governed by the Sacred Congregation of Propaganda; the Eastern rites (and the faithful of the Latin rite in many Eastern dioceses) by the Sacred Congregation for the Eastern Church. All others come under the Sacred Con-

gregation of the Consistorial with reference to the Sacred
Congregation of Extraordinary Ecclesiastical Affairs when
dealings with the civil authorities are involved.

A DIOCESE TODAY

In the ordinary way, the diocese is a fixed area, defining
the extent of the jurisdiction of a resident bishop. Apart
from exceptions laid down by general canon law or by a
decision of the pope (who has episcopal and immediate
authority in the whole inhabited world), the one bishop
is the pastor of priests and people, having also the charge of
those who do not yet form part of Christ's flock, but for
whom he accepts responsibility in the love of all souls.
He may be helped by an auxiliary bishop, or by a coadjutor who will succeed him when he can no longer perform his duties. But as there is one husband for one wife,
one baptism, one Christ, so there is but one bishop for a
diocese.

In our days, however, there are some episcopal juris-
dictions which do not coincide with a territorial boundary,
but apply to persons. There is, for example, the bishopric
of the forces, as it is called in the United Kingdom, having
jurisdiction over service personnel and their dependents,
and elsewhere the same practice applies.

In France there is the *Prélature de la Mission de France*,
with its seat at the abbey of Pontigny (Yonne), whose
prelate is Cardinal Liénart, bishop of Lille. It has its own
incardinated clergy, though they are for the service of
dioceses in special need of priests in the more difficult
fields of work. The Constitution *Exsul Familia* is concerned with the evangelization of emigrants according to
their nationality. There are also the Eastern Rites, constituting a power of jurisdiction which, as in the other

situations we have indicated, does not supersede that of the bishop of the place.

PARISHES AND RURAL DEANERIES

The territory of each diocese must be divided into parishes (can. 216). The bishop can erect new parishes, as often happens when there is an influx of population into new centres especially into the suburbs of towns. What anxieties he undergoes in trying to establish places of worship, to build halls, schools, presbyteries!

As a rule, the diocesan territory will be divided into districts, each composed of several parishes and called deaneries. (Canon Law makes no distinction between a *rural dean* and an *archpriest*: in France an archpriest is usually, but not always, in charge of an *arrondissement,* the rural dean of a *canton,* but in some dioceses all deans are called archpriests.) Canonically, rural deans are "vicars forane" (can. 217), and their position is of the first importance. Can. 445 to 450 speak of the obligations and rights of these men, who are truly the bishop's delegates (though always removable). This is no empty title for a function which in our days is admitted to be capital in combined pastoral work. The parish, centre of religious and church life, is certainly an irreplaceable entity. But just as the family cannot do without civil and religious society, so the parish is too limited to be self-sufficient. If it is not to decay and even disappear, it must be united to the Church and its immediate head, the bishop, informing him of the needs of its various elements, receiving from him the directions enabling it to continue its necessary mission. No doubt, as we shall see, there are *missi dominici,* the specialized liaison officers, the vicars-general and diocesan chaplaincies of Catholic Action, and the directors of

organizations. But certainly, to inspect the parishes and
the churches, to visit the priests, especially in their presbyteries, to bring them together and enliven their meetings,
making them more alive and brotherly than the ruri-
decanal conferences (which have long existed and too
often been abandoned), there must be a priestly soul, a
"man of God", understanding the needs of his colleagues
and of the whole region: there must be a dean. A bishop
once asked his priests to send him their suggestions for
improving evangelization and received this pregnant hint:
"We say in the prayer for vocations: Lord, give us priests.
Couldn't we add: Lord, give us archpriests?"—or, as we
should say, rural deans.

THE DIOCESAN CURIA

The bishop cannot administer a diocese by himself,
unless it is very small, and even then he will find it very
difficult. According to Canon 363, the diocesan curia is
composed of those persons who assist the resident bishop
(or whoever holds his place) in the government of the
whole diocese. It is not a corporate body, nor a college
having a moral personality. The term indicates all who
work with the head of the diocese, by acting for him in
the administrative or judicial department.

The code of Canon Law names the vicar-general, the
officialis, the chancellor, the promoter of justice, the defender of the bond, the synodal judges and examiners
(called pro-synodal if they are appointed outside the synod,
after advice from the cathedral chapter), the notaries, the
couriers and the apparitors. Clearly, in most dioceses
many of these posts are neither important nor onerous.
We should note that, unless their mandate has expired,
all these members of the diocesan curia retain their offices

during the vacancy of a see. There is only one exception to this: the vicar-general.

THE VICAR-GENERAL

The vicar-general is simply one with the bishop. When the bishop ceases to rule the diocese, his chief minister *ipso facto* lays down his office and has no further power. He may, moreover, be removed freely and without formality by the bishop, being appointed *ad nutum* and holding office according to the bishop's choice. Constituting with the bishop "a single organ of administration", he would be acting against justice and loyalty if he used his powers against the bishop's will. He may have differing and even opposed views, in which case he will offer his resignation and, although the post of vicar-general is not a benefice, equity and gratitude will find a way to use the services of a priest who is usually outstanding and experienced.

Canon 366 lays down that whenever the good administration of the diocese requires it the bishop must appoint a vicar-general to be his assistant for the whole diocese, with ordinary jurisdiction. It follows that a vicar-general is not an absolute necessity, but one is usual even in small dioceses. In virtue of his office he has precedence over all the priests of the diocese. The code of canon law only mentions one in each diocese, but exceptions are provided for by can. 366, sect. 3, where more than one rite exists or a diocese is exceptionally large.

Although the bishop alone makes nominations to this office, he will be wise to surround himself with well-informed counsellors. The full employment of the clergy is an extremely important question, both for the priest himself and for the care of souls. It is a grave responsibility for the father of his priests, who considers his duties to them even before his task of ensuring the religious life of the parishes, the different sectors and spiritual centres of the diocese. He has to prevent the sclerosis resulting from a prolonged priestly ministry in one place, and yet to avoid a too frequent change of priests, who have begun a ministry which must have a certain continuity if it is to be fruitful. The diocesan administration is sometimes accused of being heartless. But changes are sometimes postponed for motives of health and even family reasons, as for example if aged parents could not easily stand being uprooted. Then, too, the reasons for a move are not always to be made known to the public, or even to colleagues, for not being in full possession of the facts they may be less discreet than those who know them. Clerical discussions about appointments are sometimes well-founded, for everyone makes mistakes sometimes, but often things are said quite contrary to the facts. Those who talk most are not always the best informed, or the most charitable. One must say something at clerical meetings! It would be much better, however, to say it directly to the bishop, respectfully and humbly. If one is offered a post, it is well not to reveal the secret, so that the man who eventually accepts it, sometimes at considerable sacrifice, may not be lowered in the eyes of his future parishioners, or of the faithful who will be under his care.

THE CHANCELLOR

The chancellor, of course, does not manage the diocese. His immediate task is to countersign the administrative acts of the bishop and affix the seal which authenticates them, as also to see to the preservation of the archives and the church registers, the duplicates of which have to be sent every year to the secretariat of the diocese or archdiocese. Under the concordat in France, he was called the secretary-general.

When the diocese is large, one man alone cannot cope with all these tasks. He is then assisted by additional secretaries, the archivists, who inscribe the notifications of ordinations and marriages in the baptismal registers, keeping in order what is often a most valuable collection of historical documents. From him the bishop will have to obtain part of the information which enables him to present to Rome the very detailed five-yearly report on the state of the diocese, on his official visit *ad limina*, to the "threshold of the apostles".

May God grant that he and all his colleagues of the curia, or let us rather say the "bishop's household", may be able to exercise a direct ministry. It will help the development of their souls as priests and tend to balance their busy lives. Then, too, how their colleagues in the ministry love to be helped out by a member of the bishop's staff! But it must be remembered that this staff is not numerous, and service must be given on the spot, even if it means cancelling a less well-attended Mass.

THE OFFICIALIS

The bishop is an administrator in spiritual and to a lesser extent in temporal matters. But more, he is a judge. While he cannot delegate to another his function as legislator, either in the diocesan synod (which ought to meet every ten years), or in the ordinary course of events, there are great advantages if he does not normally reserve to himself the exercise of judicial authority. It is the *officialis* who performs this task in his place. Being president of the diocesan tribunal, he ought not to be the same person as the vicar-general, who oversees the administration. There is only one "official" for each diocese and he remains in office even after the jurisdiction of the bishop who appointed him comes to an end; he can be removed only by that bishop or his successors. A *vice-officialis*, or even several *vice-officiales*, may be appointed to assist him, and they are all assisted by judges, whether synodal or pro-synodal.

The promoter of justice has a special function when there is a question of public order, or of persons who have lost the right to initiate an action, such as guilty spouses whose offences have disqualified them from seeking a declaration of nullity of their marriage. It is not his business to listen to the grievances of those who imagine that justice has not yet been done to them.

In cases of ordination and marriage, the defender of the bond intervenes. His duty is to vindicate the prescriptive rights of the sacrament or contract until the contrary is proved.

What wonderful stories are told about "cases proceeding at Rome", how for payment of a vast sum an annulment of a marriage can be obtained! Of course, those who can afford to pay for the judicial expenses ought to do so, but in fact the cases of the poor (admitted without payment) succeed more often than others. Nor is one obliged to have recourse to the Holy See, to the tribunal of the Rota, first instituted in Avignon when the papacy was residing there. When anyone believes he has good reason to have a marriage declared null which really was invalid, even if the parties did not know it on their wedding-day, he presents a request, called a *libellus*, to the *officialis* of the diocese where the marriage took place, or that of his domicile. The *officialis* examines it and, if he accepts it, a minute examination follows, with hearings of the parties and the witnesses, either directly or through rogatory commissions. After intervention by the advocate and the defender of the bond, sentence is pronounced by a tribunal composed of three judges. If it concludes for the nullity of the marriage, it is necessary, but also sufficient, for a concordant sentence to be given by the appeals tribunal. For suffragan dioceses, this is the tribunal of the archdiocese; for archdioceses and dioceses directly subjected to the Holy See, another diocesan tribunal appointed once for all. Recourse to Rome is only necessary when the first decision (if in favour of nullity) is not confirmed on appeal. Ten days after the promulgation of the second sentence agreeing to the declaration of nullity, the parties are free, for their marriage had been only apparent; it was vitiated by some flaw in the form or by some diriment impediment.

It is different with unconsummated marriages. Only the pope can grant a dispensation for these. It is the Sacred Congregation of the Sacraments (or of the Holy Office, if one of the parties is not a Catholic) which gives permission to investigate the cause. All the findings are sent to the Holy See, which has to decide on these conjugal unions, which rank as valid but incomplete (i.e. not indissoluble).

While the work of the diocesan tribunals is mostly confined to matrimonial cases, their competence extends to the whole judicial field. Clerics have the privilege of not being canonically subject to the civil tribunals. To cite them, and especially bishops, before these courts would involve the faithful in the severest penalties, even excommunication. Intervention of the synodal judges and consultors occurs when a difficulty arises about the removal or recall of parish priests, movable or immovable.

THE CHAPTER

Except for some rare cases concerning the alienation of property, the consent of the cathedral chapter is not required for episcopal decisions, but more often than not its advice is sought, with good reason. Is it not the bishop's senate? He may be young, barely thirty years old and usually a native of another part of the country. The canons of the chapter are generally fairly old, and qualified to ensure a certain continuity between bishops. It is natural, too, that they should be consulted about the nominations of their colleagues and of honorary canons, though the bishop is not actually bound by their opinion. When the see falls vacant, the choice of the vicar capitular is in their hands, if there is no administrator apostolic.

In normal times, they render the public worship of God with special solemnity and efficiency at the time of their monthly meetings. In the name of the diocese they offer up to heaven the official praise, enshrining the offering of the Holy Sacrifice. It is at such times that some part of the Divine Office is recited in common.

It is to be hoped that liturgical progress will cause the importance of the Divine Office to be better appreciated, not only in religious houses, but in the cathedrals, those monuments of the faith of our fathers. The cathedral is the mother church and mistress of all the other churches and chapels. There the bishop's throne is installed, with his pulpit and the high altar. There, by preference, holy Orders are conferred. All the more reason for the priests to return there gladly. Religious communities, too, and the faithful should often pray there and take part in the pontifical Masses, sung on festivals by the bishop, surrounded by his venerable brethren of the chapter, successors of the ancient *presbyterium*.

We would make special mention of the one Mass of
Maundy Thursday morning, the Chrismal Mass, when the
holy oils are consecrated, to be used throughout the year
by the bishop's fellow-workers. If the priests now come
so willingly to this supremely "churchly" and corporate
service, it is a pity that their ministry prevents them from
taking part personally in other pontifical Masses. The
first part of such a Mass takes place at the throne. The
bishop is accompanied by an assistant priest and two
deacons of honour, while the epistle and gospel are sung
by the subdeacon and deacon of the Mass. Then the
bishop, as Doctor, usually preaches the sermon himself.
If the preacher is one of the clergy, he does not begin till
he has asked the bishop's blessing, which is as it were
a delegation of what is strictly the bishop's ministry. At
the Offertory which follows the singing of the Creed, the
complete priest, the "high priest", stands at the altar,
censing it, ascribing all honour and glory to the Holy
Eucharist, the fruit of which is the unity of the mystical
Body. It is to emphasize this that the communicants,
before receiving the sacred Host from the hands of the
celebrating bishop, first kiss his pastoral ring, which he
wears as Spouse and Pastor of his Church. The rite ends
with the triple blessing by the bishop. He blesses, in fact,
three times, either with his hand or with the monstrance,
whereas the ordinary priest, if he blesses in the bishop's
presence at the end of a Mass, does so once only, after
bowing profoundly before him as the dispenser of blessings
in the diocese. Sometimes, in virtue of a privilege, the
solemnity of the pontifical office ends with the papal blessing, given in the name of the Supreme Pontiff and con-
veying a plenary indulgence.

THE BISHOP IN HIS DIOCESE, RESPONSIBLE FOR THE APOSTOLATE

"He who listens to you, listens to me; he who despises you, despises me" (Luke 10. 16). These words refer in the first place to the successors of the apostles. Let us apply to them the words of our Lord:

> Whoever, then, hears these commandments of mine and carries them out, is like a wise man who built his house upon rock; and the rain fell and the floods came and the winds blew and beat upon that house but it did not fall; it was founded upon rock. But whoever hears these commandments of mine and does not carry them out is like a fool, who built his house upon sand; and the rain fell and the floods came and the winds blew and beat upon that house, and it fell; and great was the fall of it (Matt. 7. 24-7).

Is this not the explanation of so many abortive efforts, of "hearts slow to believe" (Luke 24. 25)? It is the bishop who has inherited the apostolic mission: he is the envoy, the missionary, in the full sense of the word.

Modern bishops do not shut themselves up in their studies, even though they realize the duty of "searching the Scriptures" and widening their knowledge of sacred doctrine and secular questions. They must "keep the faith" by fighting the good fight. Are they not responsible before God and before the pope for the apostolate in their dioceses?

Spending themselves freely, they sow the good seed, not only during allocutions in the numerous ceremonies over which they preside in the Church, but almost everywhere and always. Modern transport facilities enable them to move about and to give, by their spoken word, more vivid confirmation of the orders given in writing. Our dioceses are mostly too large for the bishop to be able to be present everywhere at once. Nor is it desirable that he should, for he must save himself for his teaching office, for the transmission of the great doctrines of the revealed message, of the providential measures of a general kind promulgated by the universal Church, and to exercise in his own person the power of teaching and guiding. Though he has the right to dispense from the laws of fasting and abstinence, it is well understood that he cannot go against the general laws of the Church. The new code of rubrics, promulgated on July 26th, 1960, gives the bishop a larger share in the ordering of the liturgy in his diocese. He is no longer merely the guardian of the law's observance, but its soul, taking into account the needs and opportunities of his people, especially as to the prayers and intercessions he may order.

As St Thomas points out (*Summa Theol.* IIa-IIae, qu. 184), the chief pastor of the diocese has, to help him, his fellow-workers who have also, in dependence on him, charge of souls. Enjoying his confidence and receiving a part of his authority, the directors of organizations, the diocesan chaplains and those of sectors of Catholic Action transmit his wishes and directions. In touch with the national chaplains, inspired by the episcopal commissions which study the problems on the larger scale of the country and the region, they know themselves to be charged with a mission to the laity and to their colleagues. With tact and delicacy, understanding and sharing local difficulties, they make themselves "all things to all men", as the bishop should be and would wish to be. "We bishops, you see," St Francis de Sales remarked, "must never refuse ourselves to anyone, if we would do our duty. We must be like those big public watering-troughs, where everybody has the right to draw water."

Standing in the place of Jesus Christ, the "universal brother", the bishop is concerned with everything in man, everything human. Guardian of sacred art, and bound to promote the Church's music and song, especially the Gregorian chant, he encourages all manifestations of art, for beauty is a reflection of God. Teacher of Christian doctrine, he protects the schools of all grades in his diocese, while praising the efforts of those who teach the truth and work on scientific discoveries. Having to remind men of the social doctrine of the Church, he lends his support to achievements more in conformity with justice and charity in the pursuit of the common weal. If he presses for the application of the Incarnation and the Redemption through Catholic Action, he invites the laity to engage in temporal action, following out the plan of Creation. God said: "Increase and multiply", and the sacrament-contract of marriage is the foundation of a fruitful, stable and exemplary home. Father of souls, he urges parents to fulfil their difficult but magnificent task, in defending and extending the unalterable rights of the father and mother over the upbringing and education of their children.

Party politics will find no adherent in him, for he is the pastor of all men, but he reminds them of their civic duty, their obligations to their country and the human family.

Gladly would the bishop repeat, first to his priests, then to all his people, the burning words of St Paul: "You may have ten thousand schoolmasters in Christ, but not more than one father: it was I who begot you in Jesus Christ, when I preached the gospel to you" (1 Cor. 4. 15).

CHAPTER IX

A BISHOP'S LIFE

The laity, and sometimes priests too, are moved by a legitimate curiosity as to the details of a bishop's life. Many see the members of the hierarchy only during solemn ceremonies or from a distance. They wonder if they are like other men, or so different that one could wish they were closer, in their manner of life, to their clergy and people. With perfect frankness, for there is nothing to hide, we shall speak of that simple and basically austere life our bishops lead.

HOW A MAN BECOMES A BISHOP

Everyone wonders about this. Is there a training-school for future bishops? Not at all. True, many have studied at the Roman universities, where they have won doctorates or licentiates, or at other great ecclesiastical colleges, or a public university. All have been through the most advanced studies in theology, philosophy, scripture, canon law, liturgy and history, in a seminary where they have been trained in piety and the duties of a shepherd of souls. Then after long years of ministry in a parish, a college or junior seminary, a chaplaincy, a higher seminary or on an episcopal staff, they have been raised to the episcopate. A long and minute inquiry, under the seal of secrecy of the Holy Office (violation of which incurs excommunication reserved to the pope, except in the hour of death), has examined the moral character (but not the social or family status), virtues and zeal of the candidate. All this has been forwarded, through the apostolic nuncio (or delegate), to the Sacred Congregation at Rome responsible for examining these cases. For the world in general, it is the Consistorial Congregation; for missionary countries, it is the Congregation of Propaganda or of the Eastern Churches; for countries where the government is involved, the Congregation of Extraordinary Ecclesiastical Affairs, whose Prefect is the Cardinal Secretary of State.

When all is ready and approval obtained—objections are rare—the newly elect is informed, usually through his bishop, that the Holy Father intends to appoint him bishop of X. on a certain date. The acceptance has to be sent to the representative of the pope, unless there are reasons for refusal, as sometimes there are. But often the supreme authority insists on the charge being accepted in a spirit of obedience. Silence must be observed until publication in the *Osservatore Romano,* which is quickly followed by announcement in the press and on the radio.

So now Monsignor, Canon or Father N. is bishop-elect of X. He is addressed as "His Excellency". He now has precedence over abbots and prelates who are not bishops, he will wear the insignia of a bishop, the purple biretta and skull-cap, the green cord on his hat, but not before he is consecrated the cross and ring or, naturally, the mitre and crozier. He must get ready for the consecration, prepared for by a retreat, which he knows to be so necessary. At the beginning of this the apostolic mandate will be read to him, one of the three Bulls giving him the right to choose as consecrator any bishop in communion with the See of Peter.

And then what worries he has, less lofty but very absorbing! There will be a vast correspondence to deal with, for telegrams and letters arrive from all quarters. Information about the diocese has to be obtained. He has to arrange and leave in good order the affairs of the ministry he has occupied. Often he is very sorry to leave it, and the friends and faithful to whom he was attached. From the material point of view, there are so many objects and belongings to be obtained! A list might interest some readers: cassocks with crimson piping; purple cassocks and fringed girdles of the same colour; a purple cloak and gloves for certain occasions (bishops belonging to a religious Order keep the Order's colour); choir habit, i.e., rochet with red apparels as on the alb, mozetta, *cappa magna, mantellettum,* green and gold cord and a chain for the pectoral cross; mitre (precious, golden and simple); tunicles, gloves, stockings and sandals of each colour for pontifical Masses; ring, crozier; ewer, candlesticks, salver, cruets for the holy oils; books, *viz.,* Pontifical, ceremonial of bishops, episcopal canon. What a mass of vestments and insignia, as costly as they are numerous! "Why have we not been content with the simplicity of the apostles?" is the heartfelt cry of their latest successor.

He will have armorial bearings devised, as far as possible in conformity with the rules of heraldry, and they will be surmounted with the cross and the hat with twelve green tassels. (An archbishop has a double cross and twenty tassels; a cardinal has twenty-seven red tassels.) There is no crozier or mitre on a bishop's arms. He will choose a motto, expressing a programme or indicating the source of his confidence amid the difficulties he foresees. Then, too, what a business it is to arrange the removal and the furnishing, if the bishop's house—don't call it a palace —is not furnished.

At last comes the consecration, often conferred by his former bishop, who both rejoices to hand on the episcopate and grieves at losing a fellow-worker and companion. His colleagues and relatives are full of pride, even if they are sad at the thought of separation. A man does not think too much about it on the day of the great ceremony, when three bishops lay their hands on his head, in the presence of their colleagues and of numerous representatives of the clergy and faithful of the diocese which is losing him, and of that to which he is going. So, at least, they hope, and they say so in somewhat dithyrambic speeches! The poor new bishop does not have too many illusions, but perhaps just a few all the same. He is going into the unknown. He has been told, with a hint of malice, that he will never again hear the whole truth, which is hidden from the great. Unfortunately this is sometimes correct, for them as for many others. He accepts compliments according to his temperament, telling himself that he will try not to disappoint them too greatly. And then above all, he has the grace of God, who owes it to himself to help his bishops to bear the cross—heavier by far than the gold or gilt cross he bears on his breast.

There are some pontifical Masses and farewell functions, which are always moving. Then he arrives in his new cathedral city, and there follows the enthronement, with variations according to whether the region is Christian and friendly or the reverse. Everywhere there is the crowd, which instinctively comes to see their bishop, to receive his blessing or to hear him. The religious communities are present in force. The members of the colleges and the various societies are led in. The civil authorities are there, heading the more faithful of the laity. The clergy watch and listen. Forecasts are exchanged. Prejudice is in his favour, for the Church, as a rule, chooses her bishops well.

A BISHOP'S DAY

Suppose that he is now acclimatized. Let us sketch in broad outline how the days, the weeks and the years are spent. At first, Providence usually makes things easy for the newcomer. He is not immediately shown all the thorns that lurk beneath the flowers.

The first three years seem easy. Sometimes trials are not long in appearing. But all depends on the generosity and good spirit of the diocese. There are, thank God, happy bishops. I believe that I have been one, *auspice Maria,* under the protection of the Blessed Virgin, whom John XXIII loves to invoke under the title of *Auxilium Episcoporum.*

In the second volume of his splendid work on St Francis de Sales (chaps. 32 and 33), Mgr Francis Trochu depicts the daily life of the holy bishop of Geneva. He describes the hours of solitude: mental prayer, Office, Mass: correspondence, that "heroic task": the audiences with rich and poor: the rush of business and the talks with his assistants: the journeys through the streets, to the bedside of the sick, to the prisoners; the time spent in the confessional in the cathedral, at the bishop's house, at the Visitation convent. The whole day was spent in the presence of God, it was active, living prayer. After supper, the rest of the Office, the Rosary. And in a very simple room, concludes the author, "cradled with the Angelus, Francis de Sales fell asleep with the peaceful slumber of a little child".

What a blessing for the bishop when he can fall asleep easily, taking the repose that refreshes and calms, while the angels, the monks and the nuns keep watch over the diocese and its pastor!

A bishop's day resembles that of his predecessor, though sometimes rather remotely. There are, as of old, the prayers, said by some very early, by others very late, and from time to time in the midst of distractions. In the chapel, Mass is said in private, or nearly so, but all steeped with the intentions of his beloved clergy, the religious, the seminarists, the militants, the sinners and the unhappy, the faithful. It may also be said in a parish church, a community, a college or a hospital. How we should try to unite ourselves with the Mass of our bishop, and of the pope, said *pro populo,* for his people, at least on all Sundays and festivals. Priests and the monasteries are associated with him in his breviary and in his other supplications for those whose charge and responsibility he bears.

In our days of movement, changes are frequent. A priest is seriously ill: the visit of his father in God will cheer him. If he dies, the head of the diocesan family will share the mourning of his colleagues and parishioners, presiding over the funeral, commending the soul of the departed, recalling the urgency of a replacement.

There are also pleasant circumstances that call for the presence of the shepherd: pastoral visitations, with their popular character and sometimes picturesque aspect, enabling the bishop to make contact with his priests and people. There are great solemnities, pilgrimages to Lourdes or to local sanctuaries, meetings, gatherings of Catholic Action or pious associations, visits to convents and schools, hospitals, prisons. The railways and air-lines have good customers among the bishops, travelling for an episcopal commission, or to Rome. If a car is useful for priests who serve more than one parish, it is essential for a bishop. It is his mobile chapel in which, if he does not drive himself, he can perform his devotions while travelling.

THE BISHOP AT THE END OF HIS LIFE

A day will come when he must lay down his post as watchman. Wedded to his Church, he is in principle indissolubly united to it. His love for it will move him to leave it when his powers decline, when it is impossible for him to fulfil his onerous task, even with the help of an auxiliary, or a coadjutor appointed to succeed him after his death. To him as to all men the hour will come, marked by Providence, sometimes when he least expects it.

Having received the last sacraments at the hands of the dean of his chapter, the bishop will offer his life for his flock. The room in his house where his body will be exposed, clad in pontifical insignia, will be the scene of many visits. There will be an unusually large congregation at his funeral, at which several of his fellow-bishops will join in the prayers of his own people. The five Absolutions will be sung. Then his mortal remains will be laid in the cathedral. His hands joined in the attitude of prayer, his body will await the glorious resurrection. His soul will appear before God, accompanied by the prayers of those he has so loved. There will not be large congregations at the anniversary services prescribed by liturgical law, or founded by him. But he will not be forgotten, least of all by the priests who owe their priesthood to him, by the religious, or by the best of the faithful, who will pray for his eternal crown. From heaven on high he will continue to intercede, powerfully helping his successor who will take over the torch, "the deposit faithfully preserved".

OUR DUTY AND ATTITUDE TOWARDS THE BISHOP

The Church is a mystery. The body of bishops, which perpetuates in time the apostolic college, shares in that mystery of life and unity, under the guidance of the vicar of Jesus Christ.

The sublime grandeur of the function of the pope and the bishops does not eliminate their human weakness, which lasts till death, when the earthly function ceases, to become an endless intercession. And so, while your obedience encourages them in the midst of their cares and troubles, pray for them that they may be examples to the flock (1 Pet. 5. 1–3), sanctifying themselves that they may sanctify others.

The liturgy orders special prayers to be said to mark the anniversary of the election and consecration of your bishop, as of the election and consecration of the Holy Father. You should often commend to the Lord, through our Lady, the intentions of the Church in his charge, for which one day he must render an account. You form part of his flock, which he must tend by love. Like Peter, he has been chosen because he loved Christ and his brethren. "Do you love me? . . . Feed my lambs" (John 21. 15–17). Come willingly to the ceremonies over which he presides, to his pastoral visitations. Listen to his words, and put into practice what he demands for your good, even if it means giving up your personal opinions. Believe that his first care is the salvation of the souls entrusted to him, but also the earthly happiness of all men.

No individual bishop enjoys the privilege of personal infallibility, but he has the "grace of state", in virtue of his episcopal consecration, to discern the needs of the universal Church and of his own flock. Until you have proof to the contrary, the word of your bishop should be received with a profound act of faith, just as he himself must believe in his mission.

Whether he is still active, or old and therefore more experienced, the Church which he embodies for you enjoys an ever-renewed youth. Go to him confidently. Why not write to him, signing your name, like Catherine de Hueck whose letters to her bishop have been published? Tell him things of which you have more direct knowledge, through your life in the midst of the world. He will listen to you kindly and attentively, even if your information, as frank as it is respectful, may not always be followed by the decision or the support you expect.

Realize that the bishop is often paralysed in his action by the lack of collaboration from Christians, who refuse to involve themselves. Haven't you sometimes said to yourself: What business is it of mine? Never forget, whatever your age, whatever your position, he is your Father in God, the father of all.

SELECT BIBLIOGRAPHY *32307*

In this series: BOVIS, André de, S.J.: *The Church: Christ's Mystery and Sacrament*; DVORNIK, Francis: *The General Councils of the Church*; LÉCUYER, Joseph, C.S.Sp.: *What is a Priest?*; METZ, René: *What is Canon Law?*; ORMESSON, Wladimir d': *The Papacy.*

AUGUSTINE, Charles, O.S.B.: *A Commentary on the New Code of Canon Law*, eight volumes, London and St Louis, Herder, 1929.

BATIFFOL, Pierre: *Primitive Catholicism*, London and New York, Longmans, 1931.

BLIGH, John, S.J.: *Ordination to the Priesthood*, London and New York, Sheed and Ward, 1956.

CONGAR, Y. M.-J.: *Lay People in the Church*, London, Geoffrey Chapman, 2nd edn 1960, and Westminster, Md, Newman Press, 1957.

DIX, Gregory: *The Treatise of the Apostolic Tradition of St Hippolytus of Rome*, London, S.P.C.K. (for Church Historical Society), 1938.

DUCHESNE, L.: *Christian Worship, its Origin and Evolution*, London, S.P.C.K., 1903.

JOURNET, Charles: *The Church of the Word Incarnate*, London and New York, Sheed and Ward, 1955.

KIRK, K. E. (editor): *The Apostolic Ministry*, London, Mowbray, and New York, Morehouse, 1946.

LEBRETON, Jules, S.J., and ZEILLER, Jacques: *The History of the Primitive Church*, London, Burns and Oates, and New York, Macmillan, four volumes, 1942–8.

PUNIET, Dom Pierre de: *The Roman Pontifical*, London and New York, Longmans, 1932.

SCHROEDER, H. J.: *Disciplinary Decrees of the General Councils* (to the Council of Trent), St Louis and London, Herder, 1937.

WOYWOOD, S., O.F.M., and SMITH, C., O.F.M.: *A Practical Commentary on the Code of Canon Law*, revised edn, New York, Benziger, 1957.

The Twentieth Century Encyclopedia of Catholicism

The number of each volume indicates its place in the over-all series and not the order of publication.